POLITICAL THEORY

DR BANTI KUMAR

Made with ♥ on the Notion Press Platform
www.notionpress.com

Contents

Preface

With the blessing of God we have completed this book titled 'International Politics' for the students of all Indian Universities in general and University of Jammu, University of Kashmir and Cluster University of Jammu in particular. This book has been designed according to new syllabus of B. A. I Semester Choice Based Credit System (CBCS) of University of Jammu and Cluster University Jammu. This book also provides multiple choice questions at the end of every chapter which will help the students to clear the entrance examinations. This book consists of four chapters. This book has been designed according to the need of the students so that they can easily understand the topic and pass out their class with good marks. This book uses very simple language so that students can manage their best in exams.

Acknowledgements

Firstly we would like to thanks Chound Mata, the tribal goddess of Gaddi Tribe for blessing us with a great work. We are also thankful to Prof. B. L. Sah, Ex. Director UGC-HRDC Kumaun University Nainital Uttrakhand for helping us in our research studies. We are also thankful to our parents and other family members for their moral as well as financial support. We are also thankful to our teachers Master Kans Kumar and Sh. Sishpal (Accounts Officer) for guiding us. We are also thankful to Principal Sir, all our colleagues from Govt. Degree PG College Bhaderwah and Library Staff for making available some good books in library. We are also grateful to Prof. Neeta Bohra HOD, Prof. Madhurendra Kumar, Prof. Kalpna Agrari and Dr. Hirdesh Kumar from Department of Political Science, Kumaun University Nainital Uttarakhand for their valuable teaching methods. We are also thankful to our friends including Dr. Pawan, Dr. Bhumika, Dr. Anita, Dr. Kailash and Dr. Sumit for their friends company. Last but not least I am very thankful to our parents and other family members for moral as well as financial support especially our son Advik and Devansh for their valuable smile.

CHAPTER ONE

POLITICAL THEORY AND POLITICAL SCIENCE

Introduction to Political Science, Politics and Political Theory.

Politics: The English word '**politics**' originates from three Greek words **polis, Polity** and **Politeia**. The word **polis** means city-state, **polity** means government and **Politeia** means constitution. In broad sense the term 'Polity', 'Politics' and 'Political' deals with the study of government and constitution of the Greek City State. The Greek City-States were relatively small communities which were separated from each other by geographical barriers, like forest, mountains and seas. Each city state had evolved a compact culture where all the institutions and activities were knit together.

The aim of these institutions was to secure **a good life** for the community of people living in these city states. In those days the term politics covered a broad meaning. In contemporary word the term politics is used in its narrow sense. Today we draw a distinction between public and private. The decisions of parliament and cabinet, decisions of political parties, their ideologies, voting behaviour, political culture etc covers the field of politics.

During the time of Plato and Aristotle the word politics was used mostly. With the passage of time, this word developed in the form of **Political Science**. The word **'Politics'** was first of all used by Aristotle. He is also known as father of Political Science.

Definitions:

Garner "Politics begins and ends with state"

Lasswell and Kaplan: "Politics is study of the shaping and sharing of power"

David Easton: "Politics is defined as the authoritative allocation of values that are binding on the society".

Paul Janet: Politics is that part of social science which treats the foundation of the state and the principles of government.

As the discipline originated and with the coming of new thinkers, new dimensions are added to it. As in the Natural Sciences there was a shift in its meaning and development from the beginning to the contemporary period in the same politics has too developed.

In the contemporary world politics is treated as an art a practical way of politics. If we say that someone is interested in politics it means he is interested in solving the contemporary problems of the society by getting elected as representative or any other method as popular in his society. We can also say that politics is an activity concerned with the welfare of the masses and development of the individual and the society.

According to the Garner the word Politics is used to describe the activities by which the public officials are chosen for making the political policies. It is confined to the business or the activity which has to do with the actual conduct of the affairs of the state.

The word political signifies something public not private. It is a decision making within and about the community. As Hannah Arendt tells that it means everything is to be decided by persuasion and not through force and violence. Aristotle says that this term not only signifies life but also the good life of the community. In classical Greece its focus was on the fundamental decision making about the affairs of the community. With the passage of time its meaning has changed.

Politics as Authoritative allocation of values: David Easton defined politics as the 'authoritative allocation of values'. In simple words authority means a legal authority i.e. a person who has the right to take decisions. Such as we have elected representatives i.e. MLA, MP or even Prime Minister or President. Allocation means distributing some rewards or some welfare scheme or even a financial reward to your hard work. E.g. we work hard before exam and sit in exam. The examiner awards us the marks depending upon our performance in written exams. Values mean economic resources or even public posts or something else valuable. So in simple language David Easton says that Politics is a process which awards the resources or even the public position to a desired candidate on the basis of his hard work through a legal authority.

Political Science: It is the science of the state or a branch of the social science which deals with the theory, organization, governments and practices of the state. Political science is one of the oldest subjects of study of the political life of man. Political science first began with the Greeks. Different thinkers have identified it with different names. Aristotle identified it with the name of **Politics, William Godwin and Marry Wollstonecraft** named it as '**Political Science**', R. G Catlin named it as '**science of state**' and Sir Fredrick Pollock named it as '**science of politics**'. Since its beginning in Greece to till date there was a change in its nomenclature but one thing is clear that it deals with the study of the state.

Definitions: Following are some of the important definitions of Political Science

Leacock: "Political Science deals with government only".

Gilchrist: "Political Science deals with the general problems of the state and government".

Garris: "Political Science deals with the origin, development, purpose and all political problems of the state".

Demock: "Political Science is concerned with the state and government".

Willoughby: "Political Science deals with State, Government and Law".

Gettel: "Political Science is the study of the present, past and future of political organizations and political theories"

It was William Godwin and Marry Wollstonecraft both husband wife who first of all used the word Political Science. Marry

Wollstonecraft was a British Feminist Philosopher and William Godwin was an Anarchist philosopher.

Since the beginning of this discipline its nomenclature as well as focus of subject has changed. There are many questions particularly from the innovative minds that being a subject of social science why it uses name science as suffix. As we know that in Natural Sciences we make use of our sense organs i.e. eyes, nose, ears and hand etc. during the experiments in the laboratory. We also make the use of these sense organs in the field of political science e.g. in order to know nature of human being and voting behaviour etc.

This is the simple reason we call it as political science. Not only political science other social sciences are also know by name of science e.g. economic science, behavioural science etc. In decentralized democracies we have Panchayti Raj Institutions which can act as a laboratory to test new political experiences such as compulsory voting, education eligibility for candidates or any other recent trend. Moreover its scope is broader than natural sciences as it is not limited to only laboratory. It has a vast practicability in this world.

Conclusion: It can be concluded that different thinkers have given different definitions according their own perspective. One thing is very clear that it is a branch of social science which deals with the study of state and other constituents within and outside the states such as human being and their influence on the state.

Political science as science

During the times of Aristotle political science was known by the name of politics and it was not an independent subject. He gave it as title to his book '**the politics**'. With the passage of time and development various thinkers gave it various names. William Godwin and Marry Wollstonecraft named it as '**Political Science**', R. G Catlin named it as '**science of state**' and Sir Fredrick Pollock named it as '**science of politics**'.

Today it is known by the name of Political Science. As we know that in Natural sciences we make use of our sense organs i.e. eyes, nose, ears and hand etc. during the experiments in the laboratory.

We also make the use of these sense organs in the field of political science e.g. in order to know nature of human being and voting behaviour etc.

This is the simple reason we call it as political science. Not only political science other social sciences are also know by name of science e.g. economic science, behavioural science etc. In decentralized democracies we have Panchayti Raj Institutions which can act as a laboratory to test new political experiences such as compulsory voting, education eligibility for candidates or any other recent trend. Moreover its scope is broader than natural sciences as it is not limited to only laboratory. It has a vast practicability in this world.

Political Science as an Art

Some thinkers have such as Bluntschi and Gettle claimed that political science is an art. Lord Bryce, Montesquieu, Bodin, Hobbes and Garner claimed that Political Science is a Science. Leo Strauss, Hacker and others recognized Political Science as Philosophy. George Sabine treated Political Science as History. Some thinkers such as Garrison are of the view that Political Science is concerned with internationalism. Almond, Powell and other American writers have studies Political Science by Sociological, Anthropological and Psychological methods. Hans J. Morgenthau recognized it in terms of power politics.

An art is defined as the practical application of the knowledge for the achievement of a desired end. Political science is a body of knowledge which can be applied to frame a constitution of a country, getting elected as a representative and making good political decision etc.

We can also understand it with an example. Various politicians studied from the Oxford, IITs, IIMs fails even to become a Member of Parliament in India. Whereas Sh. Narendra Modi the Prime Minister of India has no such formal education. He has mostly studied part time but has good art to speak for hours before public even without any written speech. This main reason behind his success is his art. So Political science is also an art.

Political Theory

To know the meaning of Political Theory it is important to know the meaning of word 'theory'. The term theory has been drawn from Greek word '**Theoria**' which means a well-focused mental look taken at something with the intention to grasp or understand it. When this approach is applied to Political field it is described as Political Theory.

Political Theory is a theoretical study of Politics like origin, nature, development, government and Political system of a State. George Sabine in his important work "**A History of Political Theory**" defined it in broad sense as anything about politics or relevant to politics. In his narrow sense he defined it as the disciplined investigation of political problems. Political Theory is all about the politics. It is an overview of what the political order is about. It is a systematic representation of what is politics. Political Theory consists of both Political Science and Political Philosophy.

Political theory deals with three kind of statements i.e.

- **Empirical statement:** It is based on observation through sense experience such as by eyes, hand and nose etc.
- **Logical Statement:** It is based on reasoning e.g. two plus two is four.
- **Evaluative Statement:** It is based on value judgement e.g. men are born free and equal.

Political Science relies only on empirical and logical statements and these statements are capable of verification. On the other hand evaluator statement changes from person to person and is not acceptable method of determining true and falls. Political Philosophy deals with the Evaluative statements.

Political Philosophy

It is the classical form of Political science. It deals with the ideal. It is normative as it deals with good and bad. Plato is considered as father of Political Philosophy as he had given various utopian concepts such as Ideal State, Communism of Wives and Philosopher ruler etc

Definitions: Following are some of the important definitions of political science.

David Held "It generally aim to explain political things coming out of political life"

Sabine "Anything about politics or relevant to politics"

Sabine "Disciplined investigation of political problems"

Bluhen: "Political Theory stands for an abstract model of Political Order".

Andrew Hacker: "Theory in ideal term is dispassionate and disinterested. As a science it describes political reality without trying to pass judgement and as a philosophy it will describe rules of conduct which will secure good life for all of society".

Brecht: "Explaining is the function of theory".

David Smith: "Political Theory is the most encompassing of intellectual activities".

A. N. Dragnich and J. C. Wahlk: "Political Theory includes philosophy, art and Politics".

S. P. Verma: "Political Theory is the outcome of a peculiar set of historical circumstances has a significant for all times to come".

Types of political theories: Political theories are of three different forms as shown below

a. Normative or Prescriptive or Classical Political Theory
b. Modern or Empirical or Descriptive Political Theory
c. Contemporary Political Theory

Classical Political/Normative/Prescriptive Political Theory: This type of theory in general way, suggests the mode by which an imperfect political or social order could be made perfect. Philosophy dominates the classical tradition of political theory. It manly focuses on the ideals or values like good, bad, just, unjust, freedom, harmony and Unity etc. The philosopher believing in classical political theory are known as radical thinkers as they believe in changing the present whole political system with a hope of establishing a ideal system. Various thinkers such as Plato, Hobbes, Lock, Rousseau and Bosanquet etc. falls in this type of political theory.

Modern/Empirical/Descriptive Political Theory: Science and its methodology dominate the modern Political theory. It is primarily concerned with the things like state structure and political process etc.It is empirical and scientific. It is based on empirical approach as use of sense organs such as mouth, nose, eyes, hand and ears is its foundation. Various thinkers such as David Easton, Robert Dahl, Graham Wallas and Max Weber etc. fall in this type of political theory.

Contemporary Political Theory: It is intended to offer an explanation of what politics is all about, a general understanding of the political word.It attempts to synthesis the essence of both the classical and modern political theory. It places more focus on the research. It focuses on majority of contemporary issues such as power politics, Political system, political culture, political socialization environment, terrorism and globalization etc. Michel Foucault, Jacques Derrida, Gilles Deleuze C. B. Macpherson and J. F. Lyotard etc. belong to contemporary political theory.

Political Philosophy: It is the classical form of Political science. It deals with the values such as good or bad, idea, ideal things and morality etc. It is normative as it deals with good and bad. Plato is considered as father of Political Philosophy as he had given various utopian concepts such as Ideal State, Communism of Wives and Philosopher ruler etc. V. V. Dyke claims that philosophical approach is an effort to clarify thought above the nature of subject and above the nature and end in studying. Majority of the classical political theories represent philosophical approach. It denotes the efforts to arrive at truth through the use of reason. The truth sought may be normative, descriptive or prescription.

The main focus of the Plato was the idea of justice and idea of good life etc. He gave concept of ideal state which was the only creation of his reasoning power. Majority of classical political thinkers begins with the hypothesis about the nature of man.

Aristotle makes his view that 'man is by nature a social animal'. Hobbes predicts the egoistic and cruel nature of human being. They gave the idea of state of nature in which human being would have lived before the formation of state. In short philosophical approach creates the knowledge based on the normative approach i.e. ideas and values which cannot be verified even in the lab of natural sciences. This approach is important as it creates the knowledge and new concepts with the help of reasoning power.

Nature and scope of Political Science

Nature of Political Science: Politics is not only a mere institution of governance but also a mechanism for achieving societal goals. Political Science is a Social Science concerned with the theory and practice of politics and the description and analysis of Political Systems and political behaviour. It includes matters concerning the allocation and transfer of power in decision making, the roles and systems of governance including governments and international organizations, political behaviour and public policies.

Political Science is thus a study of the State in the past, present and future of political organization, political processes and political functions of political institutions and political theories. Political Science has several subfields, including political theory, public policy, national politics, international relations, human rights, environment politics and comparative politics.

Being one of the oldest Social Sciences, its nature and scope of study have undergone several changes over the centuries. Various thinkers ranging from Aristotle to George Sabine and John Plamentz have tried their best to explain the nature of Political Science. Different scholars tried to claim that Political Science is Science, Philosophy, History or Sociology etc. some of the views are given below:

- Lord Bryce, Bluntschli, Montesquieu, Bodin, Hobbes and Garner claimed that Political Science is a Science. Various thinkers such as French Philosopher, Auguste Comte rejected the claim of political science as science. One this is clear that political science cannot be ranked as a science in the strict terms. But more and more effort is being made to put it in the form of social science and these efforts have increased the standard and relevance of this subject.

- Leo Strauss, Hacker and others recognizedPolitical Science as Philosophy. Various realistic thinkers such as Aristotle and Marx have criticised it because it is far away from the practical solution for a problem of world.
- George Sabine and John Seeley etc. have treated Political Science as History. John Seeley claimed that 'history without political science has no fruit and political science without history has no root'. Various thinkers such as Arthur Bentley, Charles and David Easton has criticised the political science for its more focus on history than contemporary scientific methods.
- Walter Bagehot in his work 'Physics and Politics' tried to deal with political issues with the help of psychological formulations. Harold Lasswell in his work 'Psychopathology and politics' presented a studies of politics based on psychological premises.
- Some thinkers such as Garrison are of the view that Political Science is concerned with internationalism.
- Almond, Powell and other American writers have studies Political Science by Sociological, Anthropological and Psychological methods.
- Hans J. Morgenthau recognized it in terms of power politics.

In addition to above, nature of political science also includes the following four scientific research steps

- It includes observation based on sense experiences i.e. observation based on eyes, ears, nose and skin etc.
- Generalization of these observations leading to correlation between variables.
- Framing the general rules based on correlation between variables and explaining the reason for these general rules.

- Making a Predictions based on these these general rules and prescription

Scope of Political Science: As Political Science is a very broad subject and all the day to day activities of human being are directly or indirectly covered by political science. So it becomes difficult to limit its scope. Some of the field covered by Political Science are given below:

- **Study of state and government-** It deals with the nature and formation of the State and tries to understand various forms and functions of the government.
- **Study of political behaviour of man-** Since the times of Aristotle studying the nature of human being is given more importance. Aristotle said "Man is by nature a political Animal". Political Science studies the political behaviour of man as it is important for applying a suitable system of governance. E.g. Indians, Arabian, Russian, Chinese cannot be governed with a common system because of the different nature of their native people.
- **Study of national and international problems-** Modern demands of defence of territory, representative government and national unity have made Political Science not only the the science of the political independence but also that of state sovereignty. It studies various national as well as international problems such as war, environment issues, globalization and human rights etc.
- **Study of regional organization**: It studies the regional organizations such as SAARC, ASEAN and BRICS etc. which provides cooperation to each other in different fields. Study of regional organization and research on them is important to know about their contribution in the service of humanity. Having good regional organizations can abolishes the conflicts and hence reduces the burden on international organization such as UNO.

- **Study of associations and institutions-** It studies the associations and institutions in the state as well as world. It is important to study the institutions so as to know which institution is stable and which institution is unstable. With the study and comparison we can improve our institutions and associations. E.g. institution of democracy was proved to be more stable in India as compared to Pakistan and with the communist system the People Republic of China moved far away from India in economic terms.
- **Study of the past, present and future of development**- Like history political science too studies the past, present and future of the state and factors affecting the sovereignty of the state. Study of past gives us knowledge about our pace of civilized development. We compare it with the knowledge from the study of present. With the study of present and past we can predict the changes going in future. With this we can make ourselves ready to accept the changes of future.
- **Study of the concepts of power, authority & influence**: With the behavioural revolution the central topic for study of political science have changed and become the study of power. Consequently the scope has widened to include new aspects like political socialization, political culture, political development and informal structures like interest and pressure groups. It studies the location of power in the state and various factors affecting the transfer of power from one authority to another.

Traditional Approaches to the study of Political Science: Philosophical and Historical

Approach: *An approach may be defined as the way of looking at, and then explaining a particular phenomenon. According to the* ***George Simpson*** *an approach 'consists of criteria employed in selecting the problems and data for investigation'. Ranging from birth to death of a human being all the activities and phenomenon are governed by Political Science. It is for this reason that approaches to the study of politics are so many. Broadly classifying there are two types of* *approaches to Political Science:*

a. Traditional/Normative Approach

- Philosophical Approach
- Historical Approach
- Legal Approach
- Institutional Approach

a. Modern Approaches

- Behavioural Approach
- Post-Behavioural Approach
- System Approach
- Structural Approach
- Political Economy Approach
- Dependency Approach
- Communication Approach
- Decision Making Approach
- Conflict Approach
- Group Approach
- Marxian Approach

Traditional Approaches: All the approaches in Political Science which dominated the world before the world war 1st and beginning of behavioural approaches in Political Science are known as traditional approaches. They are also known as classical or normative approaches. They mainly focus on the ethical value and are unaware about the empirical methods in politics. It is mainly classified into four types.

- **Philosophical Approach**: This approach is the oldest for the study of Political Science. In this approach the study of state, government and man is linked with the pursuit of certain goals, morals, truth etc. It is also known as idealist approach as it is based on personal thinking without any scientific proof. This approach too studies the current problems but it offers the solutions which are mostly utopian and hence not applicable. Plato gave various solutions such as philosopher ruler, communism of wives, property and children, education system to the Greek problems during his time. These suggestions of the Plato were so idealistic that it was impossible to apply them. He himself admits that there is no wrong with his concept but they are ideal and hence need ideal citizens to apply these concepts. This approach is linked with idealism. It deals more with the morality, good, bad etc. This approach takes big issues into consideration. Such issue which cannot be solved with scientific approach can be solved by philosophical approach. Philosophical approach creates new knowledge and the scientific approach tests these new ideas with the help of sense organs. Such as Karl Marx gave his concept of scientific socialism but he too used the ides as developed by classical or utopian socialists. Most of the classical theories represent the philosophical approach. They begin with some hypothesis such as nature of human being, concept of good life, Justice and political obligations. This approach was applied by Plato, Rousseau, Kant, Hegel, Green, Hobhouse and Oakeshott etc.

- **Historical Approach**: This approach lays emphasis on the study of historical events and factors for the proper understanding of the existing institutions and prediction about the future. The political phenomenon are studied chronologically order in order to understand the growth and fall of state and sovereignty. Political Science studies the past, present and future of the state and factors affecting the sovereignty of the state. Study of past gives us knowledge about our pace of civilized development. We compare it with the knowledge from the study of present. With the study of present and past we can predict the changes going in future. With this we can make ourselves ready to accept the changes of future. This approach helps in understanding the origin and development of every political concept, institution and transfer of power. Studying the political science historically gives the stamina to the various countries still today struggling for the taste of democracy. This approach was applied by Aristotle, Hegel, Marx, Karl Popper and George Sabine. Karl Marx has explained that in every stage of history there was a conflict between those having power and those not having power. This conflict results in the improvement of the condition of the section not having the power. Karl Popper has explained it as historicism. George Sabine has used this approach in his famous work **'A History of Political Theory'.**

- **Institutional Approach**: This approach lays emphasis on the study of various political institutions such as the legislative, the executive, the judiciary and political parties etc., in different parts of the world with a view to compare them and improve the existing system. This approach is very important to know about the success or failure of an institution with respect to time and space i.e. In India democracy is working good and in Pakistan it is not working good as compared to India. China is moving fast with the communist model in terms of economic power as compared to India. To copy an institution from developed country to under-developed we must keep institutional approach in mind which studies their stability in different places. This approach was first of all used by Aristotle when he studies 158 constitutions of his time and classified govt. based his research on these 158 constitutions of different Greek city states.In modern terms it also studies the CBI, PMO, RAW, White House, Parliament, Tax Office and Education System etc.

- **Legal Approach:** This approach emphasis to study political institutions on the basis of their formal and legal structure with a view to understand political science practically. This approach treats state primarily as an organization for the creation and enforcement of law. In this approach we study the authority and its legitimacy. It focuses on the legal structures of the state especially law, courts, judiciary and parliament. Legal approach studies the political science with a legal framework. For instance legal approach to Indian politics will precedes to analysis the legal implications of the Indian constitution including the decisions of Supreme Court of India, fundamental rights, power structure and its transfer etc. This approach was applied by Jean Bodin, Grotius, Hobbes, Bentham, Austin and A. V. Dicey etc.

Modern Approaches

Behaviouralism and Post- Behaviouralism System

Behaviouralism: The contemporary thinkers in political science were not happy and satisfied with the role played by the political science in the international affairs. It is believed that economists, sociologists, scientists and other specialists played their respective roles but political scientists ignored this opportunity. They made recent changes and developed theories to suit the current problems of the world but political science remained in dark ages by focusing more on values.

American Scientists attempted to establish a separate identity of political science by focusing on real character of politics. After the outbreak of 2nd World War a section of thinkers particularly Americans criticized the traditional approaches for their failure to understand Political Science. They advocated new approaches with the application of scientific methods in Political Science. These are known as modern approaches.

Those approaches which dominated the field of political science after 1945 are known as modern approaches. There are various types of modern approaches and some important among them are Behavioural, Post-Behavioural, System, Structural, Political Economy, Dependency, Communication and Decision Making approaches. Some of them are explained below;

Behavioural Approach: It was a protest against the classical approach for degrading the relevance of political science by focusing more on values. It was a peculiar phenomenon of American political thinkers.

Its evolution can be seen in the writings of Graham Wallas and Arthur Bentley. Both of them stressed greater emphasis on the informal processes of politics and less on political institutions and government.

Graham Wallas in his work 'Human Nature in politics' claimed that human nature is not rational as claimed by the liberal thinkers. Liberal thinkers particularly the Laissez-faire doctrine treated human being as rational creature with self interest.

Whereas according to Wallas new psychologist has claimed that human being is not rational and his nature is not so easy to understand. So he stressed on facts and evidences for understanding human nature and its behaviour. He claimed that political process could be understood by analysing as to how people behave under a political situation.

Arthur Bentley in his work 'The process of Government' favoured a group approach. He favoured the sociological approach by ignoring the institutions and completely focusing on the role of pressure group, political parties, elections and political process etc.

Charles E. Merriam an American thinker and founder of **Chicago School** criticized the contemporary political science for its lack of scientific rigour. He criticised the work of historians who have ignored the role of psychological, sociological and economic factors in human affairs. In his presidential address to the American Political Science Association he pleaded to focus more on political behaviour as one of the essential object of enquiry.

G. E. G Catlin also favoured a value free pure science in political science. Harold D Lasswell in his celebrated work 'Politics: Who Gets What, When, How' also applied an empirical approach to the study of political science.

Despite such attempts by these thinkers behaviouralism was systematically developed only after world war second through the writings of American thinkers. Some of important research articles and other works which played an important role in behaviouralism approach after 1945 are

- The impact on Political Science of the Revolution in the Behavioural Science 1955 by **David B. Trueman**
- The Behavioual approach in Political Science: Epitaph for a monument to a successful protest 1961 by **Robert Dahl**
- The impact of behavioural approach on traditional political science 1962 by **Evron M. Kirkpatrick**
- The Current meaning of Behaviouralism in political science 1967 by **David Easton**
- Political Behaviour 1968 by **Heinz Eulau**

It was a shift in the study of political science from the formalism, normative, philosophical, historical, institutional and legal pattern to the political behaviour of actual actors i.e. individual, political parties, pressure group, power holders, voters and elite etc.

It focuses on the actual behaviour of human beings in a Political situation rather than describing salient features of political institutions and their legal position. In behavioural approach formal political institutions are dissolved into 'system' and processes so as to focus attention on actual behaviour of political actors.

It was a revolution in Political Science. This approach was developed after world war 2nd. It was dominated by American Thinkers i.e. Charles Merrian, Gabriel Almond, Herbert Simmon, Robert Dahl and David Easton etc.

Features of behaviouralism by David Trueman: He defined behaviouralism as the science of political behaviour whereas political behaviour includes all those actions and interactions of men and group which are involved in politics. He insisted that there are two main features of behaviouralism i.e. research must be systematic and it must place primary emphasis upon empirical methods.

Features of behaviouralism by Heinz Eulau, Eldersveld and Janowitz: They focused on empirical, inter-disciplinary and scientific study of political science. They declared four features of behaviouralism in their work 'Political Behaviouralism: A Reader in Theory and Research' as mentioned below;

a. Study of human behaviour in Political science
b. Inter-disciplinary study of political science
c. Focus on empirical research in Political science
d. Use of scientific method in the domain of political science.

Features of behaviouralism by David Easton

Easton was an American Political Scientist and professor of Chicago University was one of the pioneers of behavioural approach. He acted as president of American Political Science Association from 1968 to 1969. His Major assumptions of behaviourism as are given below;

i. **Regularities:** There are discoverable regular uniformities in Political Behaviour which can be expressed in theory like statements with explanation and prediction of such theories.
v. **Verification:** The validity of such regularities needs to be tested. Validity of these theories like statements must be testable, in principle by reference to relevant behaviour.
v. **Techniques:** It holds an important place in research. It involves methods, tools used by the researcher for interpretation of data.
v. **Quantification:** Data recoded and the statement of finding requires measurement and quantification.It is necessary because in order to finding the statements measurement should be expressed in terms of actual quantity. It is required for further analysis.
v. **Value:** As before behavioural approach the main focus was on values. The behaviouralists made a distinction between ethical evaluation and empirical evaluation. They reject the old ethical and moral values whereas support empirical values which can be tested and verified.
v. **Systematization:** Just as in medical sciences he supports research by a proper system i.e. by a method and step by step.
v. **Pure science:** He calls it a pure science as it involves empirical method and it helps in solving the problems of the people and the society.It is important to utilize the political knowledge for

the contemporary problems of human being.

v. **Integration:** He stressed that the research always must be in groups such as in groups by scientists, thinkers and mathematicians etc. It stresses the integration of political science with other Social Sciences.

David Easton calls these assumptions as "**intellectual foundation stone**".

Post-Behavioural Approach: Such political scientists, who accepted behaviouralism but at the same time, wanted to reform it, came to be known as post-behaviourist and their views as Post-behaviouralism. In 1969 Easton announced a new revolution not totally opposite to Behaviouralism but made some modification in it known as Post-Behaviouralism. Centre of origin of Behaviouralism as well as Post-behaviouralism were American Universities. **Easton** gave seven traits of post-behaviourism and described them as "**Credo of relevance**" and are given below:

- Substance must come before technique. Before applying a technique we must have knowledge about our problem i.e. substance.
- Place main emphasis on social change. Our main focus should be a positive change in society i.e. social change.
- To reach out to the real need of mankind. We should focus mainly the current and true need of mankind.
- The value played an important role in politics and research. We must give equal importance to values as well as empirical methods.
- Political scientist being intellectual of society had a major role to play. If developed properly, political scientists has major role to play as compared to other social sciences.
- Knowledge must be put to work. True knowledge must be put into work so that it can serve humanity.
- Politicization of the profession-of all professional association as well as universities.

System Approach

The system theory has its origin in natural science. It was first of all given by German biologist **Ludwig vonBertallanfy** in his work **General System Theory**. After its development through Anthropology and sociology it was applied to political science by David Easton. The study of politics by using the concept of system i.e. the study of politics as system came to be called as political system. System approach in political science originated with David Easton with the publication of his book 'The political system'.

The system approach favours an inter-disciplinary approach. According to it in order to understand a system we must have to understand the functioning of its each unit which contribute in the functioning of system. After introduction of this approach in the political science by David Easton, it was further developed by various thinkers such as Gabriel Almond and Karl Deutsch etc.

Definitions:

Ludwig von Bertallanfy "a set of objects together with relation between the objects and the attitudes".

Almond "A system means attributing a particular set of properties to interactions in society".

Easton "a set of interaction through which authorities' allocation of values is made and implemented".

Collin Cherry: "a system is a whole which is compounded of many parts an ensemble of attitudes".

Hall and Fagen: "A Political System is a set of objects together with relation between the objects and between attributes"

In the field of political science there are particularly two important system approaches. First is given by David Easton and is also known by the name of Easton's system approach or Input Output model. Second is given by Gabriel Almond and is popularly known as structural functional approach.

Easton's System Approach

Easton's system approach involves input-output analysis. The political system is analyzed in terms of what it does in the environment. The system takes input from the environment into the political system for conversion into outputs. Output is produced after analysis of the input by the political system.

His conceptual framework evolved in three phases. The first phase is represented by 'The Political System' published in 1953. The second and third phases are represented by A Framework of Political Analysis and A System Analysis of Political life, both published in 1965, one after another. He gave following attributes of political system:

- Input in the form of support and demands
- Output in the form of policies and decisions
- Regulatory Mechanisms
- Feedback
- Environment

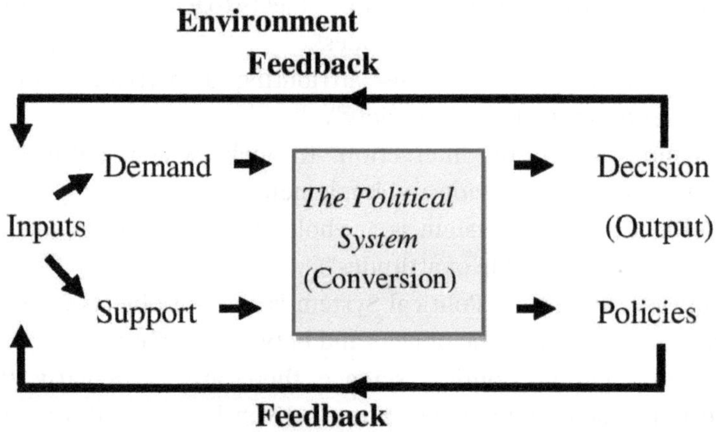

Easton's Diagram of political system

The above components of diagram are explained as below:

1. **Input:** A political system takes input in the form of support and demands. It is very important because on its basis a political system gives its demand. Demands can be following four types

    a. Demands for allocation of goods and services
    b. Demands for regulation of behaviour
    c. Demand for participation of political system
    d. Demand for communication and information

Demands have their origin either in environment of the system or within system. David Easton calls them external and internal demands respectively. Demands from social environment, cultural environment and ecological environment etc. are external demands. Internal demands can also emerge from the internal of a system to change a system itself.

Supports are those structures or processes which give the political system the capacity to cope with demands made upon it. Support means giving obedience and showing loyalty to a political system. Supports are classified into two type i.e.

a. **Overt Support:** It refers to the actions that are clearly and manifestly supportive. E.g. in India various people support by raising slogans in public or dancing on the victory of particular party in election.
b. **Covert Support:** It refers to supportive attitude or sentiments e.g. In India, government servants are not allowed to support any political party. Their social media accounts are also checked. Various people get suspend from their govt. job for their involvement in such incidents. They provide covert support to their political party by voting. It may simply involve showing smile on their faces on the victory of their favourite political party or candidate.

b. **Regulatory Mechanisms:** Every political system possesses regulatory mechanism of its own to prevent the demands from entering the system. Following are some of the regulatory mechanisms.

- **Structural Mechanism:** They are also known as gatekeepers. E.g. pressure groups, political parties etc.
- **Cultural Mechanism:** The demands against culture remain unaccepted and are not articulated.
- **Communication channels:** Demands may get scattered widely a number of communication channels and hence get diluted.
- **Reduction Process:** We have Legislatures, Executive and administrative bodies to filter demands according to their importance.

b. **Conversion process:** It is constituted by those institutions, processes and interactions by which the political system converts input into output. It can be parliament or council of a ruler depending upon the kind of political system.

b. **Output:** An output of a political system is a political decision or policy. Decision is on a particular issue and policy is a long time affect. Output is also important for the survival of the system because it has its direct affect on the public i.e. its supporters. It is dependent on the input received by system.

c. **Feedback:** Easton describes it as feedback loop. An output has its effect on the public and the public supports the political system based on its output is called feedback. It is very important because it changes the system according to the need of the people.

d. **Environment:** These are those social, biological, sociological, political, economic and personality forces, both inside and outside a particular society that affect and are affected by a political system. Some of the demands are Allocation of Goods and Services, Regulation of Behaviour, Political Participation, Communication and Information. Some of support are Material Support for (Payment of Authority and taxes etc.), Obedience support (obedience to law, rule etc) a Participation support (voting in election etc)

Some of the Characteristics of Political System as given by David Easton:

a. Political System implies a set of interactions through which values are authoritatively allocated. This makes clear that decisions of those who are in power are binding.
b. Political system is a system of regularised persistent pattern of relationship among people and institution within it.
c. Political systems likes any other natural system, has its self regulating system by which it is able to change, correct and adjust its process and structure.
d. Political system is dynamic in the sense that it can maintain itself through the feedback mechanism. It help the system to persist through every else associated it may change even radically.
e. Political system is different from other system and a boundary line separates them.
f. Input through demands and support put the political system at work while output through policies and decision enables the system to adjust itself.
g. Conversion process is constituted by those institutions, processes and interactions by which the political system converts input into output.
h. Output flow out of the political system in the form of binding and authoritative decisions, laws and policies.
a. Feedback is the process by which reactions to the output of the system travel back to the levels of inputs and give rise to activity demanding necessary outputs.

Structural Functional Approach: Structural functional approach is the derivation of system approach. It had too its journey from anthropology in the writing of Malinowski, Redcliff Brown to political science in the writing of Gabriel Almond.

This concept is basically concerned with the phenomenon of system maintains and regulation. It was hailed by some important member of the discipline as the best possible approach to the development of the theory in the field of Political Science.

It is a means which explains which political structure performance what basic function in the political system and it a tool of investigation. This method of structural functional approach was adopted in political science by leading American writers who realized that while studying political phenomenon, they should also be concerns of other things and their function in the political phenomenon.

The structural functional approach originated in the biological and mechanical sciences. It was first developed in Anthropology and after Anthropology it was applied in sociology by Talcott Pearson and Marion Levy. This approach came to the field of political science through Gabriel Almond and others.

Gabriel Almond gives a systematic definition of political system within the frame work of structural functionalism. He defined political system as an analysis which looks at political system as coherent whole which influences and in turn is influenced by environment. Almond and Coleman in 1960 used this approach in their work 'The Politics of Developing Area' to the non-western political systems.

Functions of Political system by Gabriel Almond

Almond gave four input functions and three output functions as given below

Input functions

- **Political Socialisation and recruitment:** It is the process in which we learn about our society and become a civilized citizen. Every society have different rules and and the native people follow them. It also includes political recruitment e.g. we elect our representatives MLA MP etc. for making indirect political decisions on our behalf.

- **Interest Articulation:** It is the process in which individual as well as groups make demands upon political decision makers.
- **Interest Aggregation:** It is a process in which the individual or group political demands are combined into policy programmes. In democracy it is usually done by Political Parties and Pressure Groups.
- **Political Communication:** It is simple the communication of demands as information to the political system as input, from system as output and its feedback to input. A free media is an ideal medium of communication in a political system.

Output functions

- **Rule Making:** In the democracy Rule making function is performed by the legislative organ.
- **Rule Application:** This function is performed by the executive organ of the government
- **Rule Adjudication:** This function is performed by the Judiciary organ of the government. It must be free from the clutches of legislative as well as executive organ of the government for proper development of the state.

Political Economy Approach: It is a branch of social science which studies the relationship between individual and society and between market and state, using a diverse set of tools and methods drawn largely from economics, political science and sociology.

The term political economy is a combination of two words i.e. Political and economy. The word Political is derived from Greek word "Polis" meaning city state. The word 'economy' is derived from Greek word Oikonomos which means house hold management. Thus political economy means how a country i.e. public house hold is managed or governed taking both political and economic factors into account.

Weber defines it as social science which deals with interconnection of economic and political processes. Only the Marx writers such as Paul Baran, Ander Gunder Frank and Charles Bettelheim have introduced the political economy approach while analysing the politics of Asia, Africa and Latin American system.

Paul Baran's 'Political economy of growth', Bentham's 'India Independent' and A G Frank's 'Capitalism and under development in Latin America' is notable examples of the application of the Marxist political economy paradigm to social and political change in developing countries. Gunnar Myrdal and John H Kautsky have studied the impact of economic factor on the political process of the developing countries from a non Marxist i.e. liberal point of view.

Liberal believes that private property should be protected and that of the production of wealth based on the incentive to worker and the right to property to instilled in the individual.

They suggested that individual initiative must be free from merchant constraints. Adam Smith consolidated these ideas into classical political economy. In his inquiry into the nature and the causes of the wealth of nations, he discusses the main theme of commodity and capital and values, simple and complex labour

He was the first to formulate the labour theory of value which reduces the values of commodities to the amount of labour contain in them.

Ricardo in his principle of political economy and taxation criticises the Adam Smith and advocate the accumulation of capital as the bases of economic expansion. He thought that restriction on private investment should be abolished and the governments should not intervene in the economy.

The utopian socialists like Robert Owen, Sanit Simmon and Charles Fourier critics the liberals for defending the system of capitalism by giving a twist to Ricardo's theory of labour.

Marxist and Neo-Marxist writers like Hilfarding, Kautsky and Rosa Luxamburg and others continued the radical tradition of political economy. Lenin's 'Imperialism: the last phase of capitalism' was a good example of application of political economy approach to the analysis of imperialism as a world system. Paul Baran, Leo Habberman and Paul Sweezy made a great contribution the development of political economy since about 1960.

Political economy fundamentally addresses the broad historical sweep of capitalism, especially over the past hundred years.

In Das Capital, Marx gives us the foundation of such study. Paul Sweezy in the theory of capitalist development and Ernest Mandal in Marxist economy theory interpreted Marx's findings, emphasising the economic implications. However, a synthesis by Stanley W Moore in the critique of capitalist democracy focuses on the political ratification.

Dependency Approach: It is an attempt to explain the root causes of underdevelopment of third world countries and makes the developed countries directly responsible for their under development. This model is advocated by Andre Gunder Frank, Nallestein and Celso Furtado etc.

The concept of dependency is widely used in comparative analysis of third world political system in Latin America, Asia and Africa. It evolved in Latin America in the 1960's and was later discussed in some writing about Asia and Africa as well. Both liberal and Marxist writer have propounded their own versions of the phenomena of development and underdevelopment resulting in considerable theoretical confusion about the nature of dependency and its conceptual implications.

Lenin was the first to refer to the concept of dependency as a part of his general theory of imperialism. He understood capitalist imperialism as a manifestation of the struggle among the colonial powers for the economic and political division of the world. Several Marxist thinkers explain under development of dependent countries by referring to dominants of the third world countries by monopoly capitalism. These writers argued that today corporate capitalism has replaced financial capital as the instrument of dominance in the dependent countries.

Marini has propounded the theory of sub-imperialism regarding capitalist development in Brazil. He characterised Brazilian capitalism as super-exploitive, with a rapid accumulation benefiting to the owner of means of production and absolute poverty securing to masses. His approach combined a dependency perspective with a Marxist anti imperialist framework.

A. G. Frank provides another frame work for dependency theory, he emphasised commercial monopoly rather than feudalism and pre-capitalist forms is the economy means where by national and regional metropolises exploit and appropriate surplus from the satellites. Thus capitalism own world scale promotes developing metropolises at the expenses of under development and dependents satellites. Other theorists of dependency believe that an independent capitalist development was not feasible and that instead socialism must be introduce along with a planned political economy and an intensive utilisation of natural resources. However there is no popular moment for socialism.

Communication Approach: This approach first of all appeared in cybernetics. Cybernetics is the study of the the operation of control and communication system. This approach was applied in political science by the Karl Deutsch in his work 'The Nerves of the Government: Models of Political Communication and control'. This theory regards the function of communication as the centre of all political activities. He regards the political system as the network of communication channels. It focuses on the three terms i.e. communication within the system, communication between the political system and its environment and communication between two more political systems.

This approach is very important as communication is the only process with which the two countries can go to war or peace. It is very important to know about the process of bargaining, conflict resolution, decision making and policy formulation etc.

Decision Making Approach: This approach makes a focus on the process of decision making in political process. it treats decision making as crucial and complex process in the political science.

David Easton has too given a special attention to the decision making process in his input output analysis. Decision making is a wide phenomenon. It is influenced by various factors. This approach takes into effect all those factors which influence the decision making. E.g. the distribution of the election mandate is given by the president of the party but they take into consideration all the factors including popularity, casteism and financial status etc.

The decision making approach tries to comprehend the complete process of decision making at local, national and international levels and its relation to policy formulation. There too it may cover the studies of a large variety of actors e.g. voters, elite class, political parties, legislators, judges and govt. officials etc. This approach became popular in United States. In United States there was a growing urge among the scholars to focus on decision making and government process.

Some exponents of decision making don't confine themselves to the analysis of a particular decision and proceed to undertake studies of socio-economic background of decision makers e.g. legislators, administrators, ministers, voters and pressure group etc.

Points to remember

- Plato is known as father of Political Philosophy. He was born in Greece.
- He was also known as father of organic theory.
- He was also a feminist thinker.
- He was a radical thinker as he wanted to change the system.
- Aristotle is known as father of Political Science. He was born in Greece. He was against the equality of men and women.
- Aristotle was a conservative thinker as he wanted to save the existing system by improving it.
- Aristotle believed in realistic approach.
- Machiavelli is known as father of modern Political thought.
- He separated politics from ethics.

Multiple Choice Questions

1. *Who among the following defined Political Science as 'It begins and ends with State'?*

a. *Garner*
b. *J S Mill*
c. *Machiavelli*
d. *Thomas Hobbes*

1. *Who among the following said that 'Man is by nature a social animal'?*

a. *Plato*
b. *Bentham*
c. *Aristotle*
d. *Socrates*

3. *According to Plato the population of State should be*

a. *5000*
b. *10000*
c. *8000*
d. *5040*

4. *According to Rousseau the population of state should be*

a. *9000*
b. *10000*
c. *15000*
d. *12000*

5. *Traditional Approach stresses on*

a. *Value*

b. *Facts*
c. *Objectivity*
d. *Precision*

6. *The Intellectual God father of Behaviouralism is*

a. *Charles E Merriam*
b. *David Easton*
c. *Laswell*
d. *None of the above*

7. *'Two Treatises of Govt.' were written by*

a. *John Lock*
b. *Rousseau*
c. *Hobbes*
d. *Bentham*

8. *'A right is a claim recognized by society and enforced by State' who said this*

a. *Laski*
b. *Bosanquet*
c. *Rousseau*
d. *Green*

9. *The concept of Greek's Justice was*

a. *Legal*
b. *Moral*
c. *Social*
d. *Political*

10. *Who wrote the book 'The Politics'?*

a. *Plato*
b. *Aristotle*
c. *Machiavelli*
d. *Hobbes*

11. *Who wrote the book 'On Liberty'?*

a. *J. S. Mill*
b. *Bentham*
c. *Karl Marx*
d. *None of the above*

12. *Which of the following is not a traditional approach?*

a. *Historical Approach*
b. *Legal Approach*
c. *Philosophical Approach*
d. *System Approach*

13. *Which of the following is a classical approach?*

a. *System Approach*
b. *Behavioural Approach*
c. *Philosophical Approach*
d. *None of the above*

14. *'Credo of Relevance' signalled*

a. *Modernism*
b. *Behaviouralism*
c. *Post Behaviouralism*
d. *None of the above*

15. *Integration of Political Science with other Social Sciences is a basic principle of*

a. *Traditionalism*
b. *Behaviouralism*
c. *Liberalism*
d. *Post-Behaviouralism*

Answer Key

1. (a) 2. (c) 3. (d) 4. (b) 5. (a) 6. (a)
7. (a) 8. (b) 9. (b) 10. (b) 11. (a) 12. (d)
13. (c) 14. (b) 15. (b)

Exercise for practice

Short Answers Type Questions

Q1. Define the Concept of Politics?

Q2. Examine the meaning of political science?

Q3. Define Political Theory?

Q4. Discuss Political Science as a science?

Q5. Discuss Political Science as an Art?

Q6. Give the scope of political science in your own words?

Q7. Define Political Philosophy?

Q8. Define legal approach to Political Science?

Q9. What do you understand by institutional approach to political science?

Q10. Define classical political theory in your own words?

Q11. Define Modern Political Theory?

Q12. Define contemporary political theory?

Q13. What do you understand by the term behaviouralism?

Q14. What are the basis assumptions of behaviouralism as given by David Easton?

Q15. Define Post-Behaviouralism?

Q16. Write a short note on Political System?

Q17. Explain in brief the system approach as given by David Easton?

Q18. Mention the functions of Political System as given by David Easton?

Q19. Differentiate between traditional and modern approaches?

Q20. Define decision making approach to political science?

Q21. Define communication approach to political science?

Q22. What do you understand about structural functional approach?

Long Answer Questions

Q1. Explain the nature and scope of political science?

Q2. What do you understand by the approaches to the study of political science? Discuss Philosophical approach?

Q3. What do you understand by the approaches to the study of political science? Discuss Historical approach in detail?

Q4. Define system approach? Explain in detail the system approach given David Easton?

Q5. Explain the Political economy approach to the fields of political science?

Q6. Explain the dependency Approach to the field of political science?

CHAPTER TWO

State: Origin and Nature

Meaning and Elements of State:

The word 'State' has its origin in the Latin word '**Status**' used by teutons which means 'standing' or 'position' of a person or body of persons. The concept of the State is comparatively modern and owes its origin to word '**Stato**' used by Machiavelli in his writing in sixteenth century. After used by Machiavelli in Italy it soon became popular in England and France. The concept of state occupies a central place in the political science.

No discussion on political theory is complete without reference to the word 'state'. The state touches every aspect of human life and due to this reason it has captured the attention of various legend political thinkers in political science since the days of Plato. **Ralph Miliband** in his work "**The State in Capitalist Society**" says that the government, the administration, the military, the police and judiciary sub-central government and parliamentary assemblies makes up the state. Various thinkers have given different view about State & some of them are given below:

Plato "a State is a system of relationships in which everyone does his own business and the job of the State is to maintain, and promote such relationship".

Aristotle "The State is a union of families and villages having for its end perfect and self-sufficient life".

Thrasymachus "State is no more than the rule of stronger".

Machiavelli "State is power which have authority over men"

Bluntschli "State is the politically organized national person of definite territory".

Woodrow Wilson "State is person organized for law within a definite territory".

Bodin: "A State is an association of families and their common affairs government by a supreme power and reason"

Easton "The word state ought to be abandoned entirely"

Maclver "The State in a word regulates the outstanding external relationships of men in society"

Max Weber "The state is considered the sole source of the right to use violence"

Hegel: "State is the march of God on earth"

Trietschke "The state is power"

Louis XIV of France "I am the state"

Proudhon "State is unnecessary and undesirable evil"

T H Green: "human consciousness postulates liberty, liberty involves rights and right demand the state".

Elements of State: In the present times we call Punjab a State or Uttrakhand a State, politically they are not State but only a federal part of their political State i.e. India. So politically a State has following four elements:

- **Population**: Population is very important element of State. There are no fixed criteria for the number of people in the State. There are large States such as China, India having largest population of the world. There are small population States too such as Vatican City. Plato mentioned 5040 population for his ideal State. Rousseau was of the view that population of the state should be 10,000. Whereas Aristotle was of the view that population of a State should neither be too small nor too big.It should neither be so large that administration may be a problem, nor so small that the people may not lead a life of peace and security. It should be so much that the people may lead a life of self sufficiency. Aristotle gives brilliant criteria for the population of the state. Moreover these classical thinkers have never imagined that in future this world could have states like China and India.

- **Territory**: It is also an important element of State. It is the area whether land, sea and air are under the jurisdiction of the state. There are thinkers such as John Seeley, Duguit and W. W. Willoughly etc. writers who don't consider territory as important element of the State. Aristotle the father of political science gave more importance to territory by saying that population should be according to the territory so that the people can survive from the available territorial resources. Moreover gypsies and nomadic cannot be said to constitute State. There is no fixed criterion for the size of territory. Territory can be in land form, it can be in the form of lakes, rivers or oceans. The territory of a state includes land, water and air space. It has maritime jurisdiction up to three miles, though some states such as China claims up to 20 miles. On the one hand we have states like Russia which is largest in terms of area. On the other hand there are states such as Vatican City which is smallest in size.
- **Government:** To execute the will of the State we need machinery called government. It is another essential element of State. It is the agency or machinery through which common policies are determined and by which common affairs are regulated and common interest promoted. Govt. can be of any type such as democratic, communist, dictatorship and monarchy etc. The authority of the State is exercised by the govt. Laws of the State are made, declared and enforced by government. Mainly govt. consists of three important organs i.e. Legislative, Executive and Judiciary.
- **Sovereignty:** It is another essential element of the State. Without sovereignty, there can be no State in the legal sense. It is sovereignty which distinguishes the State from other organization. It is the final authority in a State. In contemporary world particularly in the democratic countries, sovereignty lies in the hand of people.It is by virtue of its sovereigntythat a

state declares its laws and decisions through the government and issues commands which are binding on all citizens. It claims the obedience and punishes the offender.

Three different meanings of state in India

In India the word state has three different meanings i.e. in Political Science, in day to day common life and in constitution of India.

These are explained below

a. **Meaning of State in Political Science:** In the field of political science the word state means a country with its four elements i.e. population, territory government and sovereignty. So in our country politically Punjab is not a state. It has population, Territory as well as its state government but its sovereignty is limited by the Government of India. So India is politically a state but not Punjab or Haryana. Moreover India also became state after 1947 and before 1947 it was a nation not a state.

b. **Meaning State in common day to day life:** In contemporary time internationally as well as in our country the word state is commonly used to denote the federal units i.e. State of Punjab, State of Haryana and State of Uttrakhand etc. the political divisions of our country. They are integral part of territory of India

c. **Meaning of State in Constitution of India:** In constitution of India it has its separate meaning. Article 12 deals with definition of the state. It considers three bodies under it i.e.

- Government of India and Parliament
- Government of states and Legislative Assembly
- Local Self Government i.e. Panchayati Raj and Municipalities
- Any other semi government organisation such as LIC etc.

Society

Society is an association of human beings which fulfils all their need of life from cradle to grave. The State fulfils the particular need of the people. It subjects them to binding laws and decisions of the state to provide for order, security, commerce and services. Society is a primary association and State is formed out of it. There can be a society outside the State i.e. we can have a world Tiger society to save tiger with member outside India. There can be a society without a State i.e. society of nomadic tribe people who don't constitute a State.

The roots of the term society can be traced to the Latin word 'socius' which means companionship or friendship. **George Simmel** an eminent sociologists has stated that it is the element of sociability or companionship which defines the true essence of society. As Aristotle stated centuries ago "**man is a social animal".** It brings into focus that man always lives in the company of other people. Society has become an essential condition for human life to continue. Herein, we will discuss some of the views of the social thinkers on society.

August Comte viewed society as a social organism possessing a harmony of structure and function. Emile Durkheim regarded society as a reality in its own right. For Talcott Parson Society is a total complex of human relationships in so far as they grow out of the action in terms of means end relationship intrinsic or symbolic. G. H. Mead conceived society as an exchange of gestures which involves the use of symbols. Morris Ginsberg defines society as a collection of individuals united by certain relations or mode of behaviour which mark them off from others who do not enter into these relations or who differ from them in behaviour.

Nation

It refers people living in a definite territory, inspired by a sense of unity, common political aspiration, common interest and common history etc. Member of nation distinguish themselves from other nation.

The word 'nation' is derived from a Latin word 'natio' which denotes the idea of common birth or descent. In political science it denotes people or set of people inspired by a feeling of national unity based on common race, language, culture, geographical compactness etc. feeling of nationality separates people from other such nation. Love towards a nation is called nationalism.

An important quality of it is to bring together people from different social and cultural level. There is no coercive force for unity in a nation as they have we-feeling and attachment to the mother land just in their blood which keeps it united.

Some of the important definitions of Nation are

"A nation is a culturally homogenous social group which is at once conscious and tenacious of its unity of psychic life and expression" **Garner**

"The Nation underlines the state" **T. H. Green**

"A Nation is a union of masses of men bond together especially by language and customs, in common civilization which gives them a sense of unity and distinguishes from all the foreigners, quite apart from the bond of the state" **Bluntschi**

"Nation is a state plus something else; the state looked at from a certain point of view, viz. that of the unity of the people organised in one state" **Gilchrist**

Difference betwen State, Society and Nation

State	Society	Nation
It is a political association having four elements i.e. population, territory, Govt., and Sovereignty	It is a community of people bounded by common cultural and social interest.	It is an association of people bounded by a unity of nationalism.
It is a political organization.	It is a social organization.	It is spiritually organized.
It has fixed boundary.	It doesn't possess fixed territory.	It also has fixed territory.
Sovereignty is its important element.	Sovereignty is not its essential element.	Sovereignty may or may not be its essential element.
India is today a state but not before 1947.	India was also a society before 1947.	India is today a nation and it was also before 1947
Organized govt. is an important element of State	Society needs no govt.	Govt. is important part of nation.
State needs its four elements.	Society needs no element.	A nation too needs no element.
State is newer than society but older than nation.	Society is oldest of these three.	Nation is recent concept as compared to these two.
State depends upon society for its existence.	Society doesn't depend upon state for its existence.	Nation depends upon society for its existence.

Difference betwen State, Society and Nation

Theories of Origin of State

Various theories with regard to the origin of state are offered. These include the divine origin theory, the force theory, the patriarchal/materialistic theories, social contract theory, the evolutionary/historical theory and the Marxian theory. Important among them are divine origin, Historical origin and social contract theory.

Divine Theory of origin of State:

According to this theory the State is created by God himself and is ruled by him directly or indirectly through his representative on earth i.e. king. They treat king as absolute and the only source of law. He is responsible only to God. There is no empirical proof of this theory but various religious book makes mention in favour of this theory. According to **Mahabharata**, a Hindu religious epic, there was anarchy in the beginning of this world and the people approached the **Bramha** (a God among Hindus having four heads which are faced to four directions on a single body) to come to their rescue. It was under these circumstances God appointed his son Manu to rule over the people.

According to the Jews the king is treated as owing responsibility to God alone for his acts. According to Bible let every soul be subject onto the higher powers, for there is no power but of God. The theory of divine origin was used to support the theory of the divine right of kings. James I, King of England, supported the theory of divine right of king in his book '**The law of free Monarchies**'. His view was that kings were kings because God had made them kings and are responsible to God alone. The process of Khalifa among the Muslim world also indicates to proof of this theory.

This theory was popular for a long time but later on it began to decline on account of many factors such as emergence of social contract theory etc. Thinkers who supported this theory are R. Filmer, Bossuet, Saint Augustine, G. P. Gooch and J. N. Figgs etc.

Historical/Evolutionary Theory of origin of State

This theory holds that state was neither the creation of God nor the social contract. It simply supports that it is the product of gradual growth of history and various factors have played an important part in its evolution. It is the continuous development in the process of evolution. **Gettell** says "State is neither the handiwork of God, nor the result of superior physical force, nor the creation of compact, or a mere expansion of the families. It is the product of a gradual process of social development out of grossly imperfect beginning". Following are some of factors responsible for creation of State.

- **Social Instinct**: The instinct which compels man to live in the society, without which he is either a beast or a god and the one through man, is able to develop his faculties. According to Aristotle "Man is by nature a political animal". He further says "he how is unable to live in society must be either a beast or God."
- **Kinship**: It is admitted that the family was the unit of society at the beginning. The blood relation brought the members of a family together and they accepted the authority of the head of family. With the passage of time this family expended into clans, tribe and finally into State.
- **Religion**: It also played an important factor beyond the creation of State. The people who were bound by the bonds of blood were also brought together by religion. The priest or the magician was considered to have mastery over the force of nature thus they were willing to obey his authority. Moreover the emergence of the all religion i.e. Hinduism, Christianity, Islam, Sikhism, and Buddhism etc. united the people in groups. Even today also some self styled God-man i.e. Babaas, have a large number of followers with them. Moreover, modern political thinkers such as Karl Marx also highlight the importance of religion among people. He says that "religion is the opium of people".
- **Force**: It is believed that force played an important role in creation of State. The stronger ones suppressed the weaker class and ruled over them after uniting. Before the independence and the coming of East India Company we get the evidences of the King ruling by force. The weak kingdoms were defeated and were combined in powerful one. This was also the case with Mughal Empire in India.

- **Economic Activities:** The economic interest must have played an important part in the evolution of State. Since man produces in group more than in isolation, so he must have started living in groups for more production. They felt the need of a common authority and in course of time, the State came into existence. According to Professor Laski "the basic factor in any given society is the way it earns." This point can be seen in modern world such as United States of America and European Union etc. are living in common for economic and security purposes.
- **Political Consciousness:** Political consciousness among the people also brought them together. When primitive people gave up hunting and wandering habits and took to pastoral and agriculture life, many changes took place. Population began to increase more. Wealth began to accumulate. The idea of property also emerged in the minds of man. Few of them thought the need of an association to maintain law and order. This idea circulated and resulted in the formation of State because of their political consciousness.
- **Property and defiance:** Since before the creation of State, the man was wandering and was just living as a nomadic hunter. They had no property except their few hunting tools. After that they passed through three economic stages i.e. huntsman stage, pastoral stage and agricultural stage. When he started agricultural work and settled in a territory, he made a property such as utensils, clothes and surplus food grain etc. he felt the need of security to guard his property. This need resulted in the form of State, which provided security to their property. Social contract theorist such as Hobbes, Locke, Rousseau and even Karl Marx also believe in it.

Social Contract Theory of origin of State

This theory is a reaction to the divine theory of origin of State. This theory states that the State is the result of an agreement between the individual themselves who originally had no governmental organization.

Origin of this theory: There is no scientific proof of this theory. It is the creation of mind of some thinkers. Its traces may be seen in the **Mahabharata** (a Hindu religious epic) and also in the **'Arthashastra'** (a book) of Kautilya. The **sophists** and the **Epicureans** of the ancient Greece also believed in it. Roman thinker such as Polybius and Cicero also believed in it. In the modern sense it was developed by the three main thinkers i.e. Hobbes, Locke and Rousseau.

The main supporters of this theory are Thomas Hobbes, John Locke and J. J. Rousseau. Although they too differ in the process of contract, sovereignty etc. but one thing is same as they treat state a creation of the social contract. Before the formation of State, man lived in the state of nature. All the above three have given their different view about State of nature. In addition to above three latter Immanuel Kant, Herbert Spenser, John Rawls and Robert Nozick also used this theory to make their own concepts.

Thomas Hobbes view on social contract:

State of nature: It was the society in which men lives before the creation of State. Hobbes was of the view that life of man in state of nature was solitary, poor, nasty, brutish and short. Every man was enemy to every man. Nobody was able to overpower the other. Hence men stand in natural fear of each other. It was a state of total insecurity. In the state of nature there was no liberty except the liberty of each man has to preserve his own life.

Contract: In the state of nature there could be no distinction between right and wrong because of lack of judges. In state of nature the desire for gain of human being lead to violence. This violence lead to necessity for protection and its result was the establishment of a common power for protection. Hobbes quotes the contract in his word "I authorize and give up my right of governing myself to this man". He offered a single contract to merge from state of nature and establish society and state. Contract was based on reason not on fear.

Sovereignty: State of nature was characterized by anarchy and total insecurity so Hobbes therefore doesn't admit people right to revolt or revolution. The sovereignty formed was not a party to contract because it formed after contract. Hobbes postulates that State and society were formed together and are dissolved together. He offered an absolute sovereignty. He gives name to the product of his contract as 'commonwealth' and it includes state, society and government. He gives names to the monarch ruler of his state as 'Leviathan' which means a very large sea creature.

John Locke's view on social contract:

State of nature: Locke puts a different picture of state of nature completely opposite as shown by Hobbes. In his view, it was not a state of constant warfare. On the contrary, it is a state of peace, goodwill, mutual assistance and preservation. It was a State of liberty, not a state of license. The majority of the people obey the law of nature i.e. morality. But there were few minorities who set aside the rule of morality for their self interest. In the absence of established authority it was difficult to deal with such offender. He says if men become judges of their own cases, justice would not be secured. To deal with this situation state was created by social contract.

Contract: To deal with few offenders of law of morality, a social contract was done to establish a sovereign. He offered a **two step contract** i.e. social and political. The first contract lead to formation of society and the second contract lead to establishment of govt. The ruler was given to preserve right to life, right to property and right to security. If a ruler fails to provide these right, the people have right to dethrone the ruler. It was a contract of all with all.

Sovereignty: Locke recognizes the people's right to revolution if the ruler fails to provide right to life, right to property and right to security. He supported limited or constitutional monarchy.

J. J. Rousseau view on social contract:

State of nature: He states that men in state of nature are equal, self-sufficient and contend. For him, the state of nature was a **noble savage** for him but with the rise of the civilization inequalities raise their heads. With the development of arts and science, private property came into existence, which leads to division of labour. To avoid this they established the state with a sovereign by means of social contract.

Contract: In order to get rid of above situation a contract was done by surrendering the rights of everybody on the name of the community. Just like Hobbes he gives a single contract. In the word of Rousseau “Each of us put his person and all his power in common under the supreme direction of general will and I our corporate capacity we receive each member as an indivisible part of the whole”. Rousseau calls his contract as General Will.

Sovereignty: He offered an indivisible sovereignty called General will. General Will is different from real will. General will is motivated by ultimate collective will i.e. the will when one thinks of common good whereas the real will is motivated by self interest. The sovereign of Rousseau is as absolute as that of the Hobbes. The sovereignty of the state is unlimited. It is the sovereign community which has absolute and unlimited powers and not the government.

Differentiate between views of Hobbes, Locke and Rousseau

Term	Hobbes	Lock	Rousseau
State of Nature	Solitary, poor, nasty, brutish and short.	State of peace, goodwill, mutual assistance and preservation.	equal, self-sufficient and contend noble savage
Natural Rights	Oppress others and self defence	Right to life liberty and property	Liberty to fulfil needs from natural resources
Purpose of Social Contract	Powerful sovereign for control and protect	Government which will protect natural rights and punish offender	Security to the property of the people
Stages of Contract	single contract	two step contract	single contract
Sovereignty	absolute sovereignty	Limited Sovereignty	absolute sovereignty
State	State and society are created simultaneously	State and society are not created simultaneously	State and society are created simultaneously
Right to revolt	No	Yes if natural rights are violated	No

Differentiate between views of Hobbes, Locke and Rousseau

<u>**Theories of Nature of State**</u>

Various theories have emerged to explain the nature of State. Some of them are Organic theory of the state, Liberal Individualist prospective, Marxist perspective, Welfare State prospective, Communitarian prospective, Gandhian prospective, feminist perspective and Pluralist perspective etc.

<u>**Organic theory**</u>

Organic theory of State treats State as a natural institution. This theory sees the State in term of natural Sciences. According to this Theory State is formed of several individuals just as a living body composed of cells. The view of State as organic was started from the Greek. Plato compares State to a man of great structure. Aristotle was of the view that State came into existence for the sake of life, and continues for the sake of good life. Aristotle held that man by nature is a political animal.

The state is so fundamental to human existence that Aristotle declared in his typical style state is prior to man. The view of Herbert Spenser was that the State was a natural organism which did not differ much from a biological organism. This perspective of state treats individual as means and state as an end in itself. As individual organs of an organism, such as hands, feet or teeth can have no real interests of their own apart from the interest of the state.

Thus the champions of the organic theory claimed that individuals could have any rights within the state but they could never have any rights against the state. True freedom of the individual lies in the obedience to the laws of the state. Plato, Aristotle, Hegel, Marsilo of Paua and Herbert Spencer etc. are some of its exponents.

Features of Organic theory of State:

- Society is a living organism with special characteristics that obeys, as a living organism, the law of biology.
- The main mission of the ruler is to preserve the unity of the whole. This unity is possible with concord.
- As a consequence of the above, discord is the worse evil of a society.
- The emergence or development of factors that could weaken the state should be avoided at all costs.
- The govt. has, in the political field, the same function that the heart has in the human body.
- A model of organic society with excellence is the family.
- Monarchical regime serves this conception of society.
- The State lives, grows and develops much as an individual does.

- As an organism is composed of cells, so the state is composed of individuals.
- The regulatory system of organism consists of brain and nerves, govt. and Military holds the same for state.

Criticism: This theory was criticised as it makes a restriction on the individual. It makes the state an undemocratic. It is even today treated as an important in absolute monarch and some communist countries. It is not treated as an important theory in democratic world. Moreover it is against the Gandhian concept of means and ends.

Liberal Theory of State

Liberal theory of nature of State consists of classical liberal theory and modern liberal theory.

Classical liberal theory of nature of State: This theory advocates the negative nature of the State. It is also known as negative liberal theory of nature of State. Early exponents of liberalism include John Locke (1632-1704), Adam Smith (1723-90) and Jeremy Bentham (1748-1832). Locke is known as the father of liberalism, Smith is known as the father of economics and political economy and Bentham as the founder of utilitarianism. All of them defended the principle of laissez-faire which implies the least interference of the state in the economic activities of individuals.

They are the founders of Classical Liberalism which is also called negative liberalism because it envisions a negative role of the state in the sphere of mutual interaction of individuals. Locke emphasized toleration and freedom of individual conscience. Bentham emphasized the expansion of the market economy and restriction of the sphere of state activity. This theory was advocated by the Bentham, Adam Smith, J. S. Mill, Herbert Spenser, William Senior, Thomas Paine, Robert Nozek and Oakeshott etc.

Features of Classical liberal theory of nature of State

- State is necessarily evil.
- State performs minimum functions.

- Individual enjoys maximum liberty.
- It is based on free market society.
- Capitalist class is free to exploit the working class.
- The state advocates the policy of laissez-faire.
- This concept of state is advocated by the capitalist class.

Modern Liberal Theory of Nature of State: This Theory of State advocates the positive role of the State. J. S. Mill revised the classical liberalism and transferred into modern liberalism or positive liberalism. The aforementioned problem brought a new change in society, the uprising of the working class. In the 20th century the rising working-class questioned classical liberalism and its core argument to support negative liberty, i.e. laissez-faire market.

Laissez-faire individualism encouraged capitalist economy, and consequently, the working class was deprived of its due share. A new form of liberalism came up – Modern Liberalism, also known as welfarism. Thinkers of this strand of liberalism believed that government has to remove obstacles that stand in the way of individual freedom. The main exponent of this statement was T.H. Green. According to him, excessive power of government might have constituted the greatest obstacle to freedom in an earlier era, but by the middle of the 19th century these powers had been greatly reduced or mitigated.

Now, there were different kinds of hindrances, such as poverty, disease, discrimination and ignorance that could be overcome only with positive (positive liberty) assistance of government. This theory was advocated by J. S. Mill, T. H. Green, H. J. Laski, Maclver and J. M. Keynes, etc.

Features of Modern liberal theory of nature of State

- State is necessarily institution.
- It is a welfare State.
- It provides various services to the citizens especially the poor and working class.

- State controls the economic system and imposes various taxes on it.
- Citizens enjoy universal adult franchise.
- A modern liberal theory of state is supposed to be stable.
- It provides right and duties to its citizens.
- Individual enjoy minimum liberty.

Conclusion: It can be concluded from the above discussion that liberal theory of nature of State focuses on function of State in society. Classical liberal theory stresses limited role of State in the governance of society. The modern liberal theory stresses on the more role of State in protection of its citizens and providing them various social services. It can be said that Modern liberal theory was an improvement in the classical liberal theory of nature of the State.

Marxist Theory of State

According to Marxism view the State as a creation of capitalist class. The Marxist Perspective, also commonly regarded as the class theory of State, is basically a perspective, which has evolved from the writings of Karl Marx, Freiderick Engels and some other classic Marxist theorists such as Vladimir Lenin, L. Trotsky and Antonio Gramsci.

It is worth remembering here that Marx did not offer a theoretical analysis of the State as such. His work on the State comprises a fragmented series of philosophical reflections, contemporary history and journalism and incidental remarks. It is not surprising, therefore, that Marx rarely focused directly on the complex concept of State. From the beginning, Marx made it clear that the point is not to contemplate or interpret the world, or the State, but to change it. Therefore, it is difficult to acquire any clear unitary theory of the State from the diverse writings of Marx and Engels themselves.

The emphasis of Marxism has not been to understand the State in itself, but rather to explain it as a result of a more fundamental reality, which is usually economic in character. Thus, it is the functional role of the State within the economy, rather than it's Constitutional or institutional form, which is significant. In the evolution of the State he refers different stages of economic development.

Mark view State as a negative concept. They believe that State is an institution created by the capitalist to carry on their profit purpose. State has not existed from beginning; there had been societies in history where State was not known. They describe State as a result of following stages of economic development and also lists the division of society into two classes i.e. haves and have not as shown in below table.

Historical Stage	Mode of production	Class Structure
Primitive Stage	Hunting, fishing, food gathering.	Class not yet emerged.
Slave Stage	Animal Husbandry, domestic Agriculture	Master and slave.
Feudal stage	Large scale agriculture	Landlord and Serf
Capitalist Stage	Large scale industries	Capitalists and workers
Socialist Stage	Large scale industries	Workers in power

Enter Caption

Marx after explaining the historical interpretation of the economic developments predicts this stage of capitalist as the 2nd last stage to make the society stateless i.e. socialist state. In his work Communist manifesto Karl Mark appeals the workers of the world to unite for the revolution so as to convert this society into a classless society. He calls them to unite for revolution as they have nothing to lose except the chains in their hands and they have a world to win. He explains in simple words that how the bourgeois class is being benefited by the state by earning of surplus value. Surplus value is the difference between the cost paid to worker and the actual selling cost of product. This amount is totally held by the bourgeois class.

Here Karl Marx claims that the worker class has to capture the economic modes of production. Antonio Gramsi an Italian gave more preference to the other institutions such as family, school and religious institutions. He gave a concept of hegemony. When a preliterate class rules the bourgeois class and that too by the will of bourgeois class, it is known as hegemony.

The capitalist class has established a culture of accepting the coercive authority by establishing various institutions such as family, school, church which trains the citizens to accept the authority of the state. The state uses these institutions to rule the bourgeois class and uses its own coercive power only when these institutions fail to do it.

Features of Marxian State:

- Establishment of social mode of production, the objective of which will be social welfare not profit.
- Abolition of private property and establishment of social ownership of the means of production.
- Land reforms and establishment of cooperative and state forming.
- To arrange welfare services to the working classes.
- Industrial and agricultural development through the application of new scientific and technical means.
- Increasing production and enriching the material life of the whole population.
- Establishment of planned economy to organize production according to the need of society.

Sovereignty

The term 'Sovereignty' is derived from Latin word '**superanus**' meaning supreme. Thus the sovereignty denotes the supremacy or supreme power of the state. Sovereignty is a key concept in traditional political theory. It constitutes one of the four elements of the state without which statehood remains incomplete. Sovereignty as the supreme power of the state is a modern concept. It came into existence with the rise of the nation-state in Europe when the powerful monarchs asserted their authority.

But as such, the idea of sovereignty is very old and can be traced to the ancient Greek City-States. Aristotle, the father of Political Science, defined it as the supreme power of the state. But Aristotle did not discuss the nature of sovereignty. He concentrated on the location of sovereignty.

The concept of sovereignty was first of all systematically formulated by a French Philosopher **Jean Bodin**. He gave absolute sovereignty i.e. placed sovereignty above law. He treated it above law but not above duty and moral responsibility. He places two limitations on it i.e. there are some fundamental law (salic law of France) which sovereign could not lawfully abrogate and private property is granted by the natural law and hence sovereign could not tax his subjects without their choice.

After him **Hugo Grotius**, a Dutch jurist and the father of international law made important contribution to the concept of sovereignty. He made sovereignty independent from the foreign control. He gave concept of International law on two foundations i.e. Nations are subject to natural law in the same manner as citizens are subject to national law and a voluntary law of nations based upon three consent such as via treaty, conventions etc. We can say that Grotius also attributes moral responsibility to sovereignty and extends it to the external sphere.

After Grotius **Thomas Hobbes** in his social contract theory declares that sovereign is the result of the will of the people and projects the concept of absolute sovereignty based upon the negative nature of human being.

This concept of sovereignty was further modified by **John Locke**. He claims that the sovereignty is the result of the will of people but sovereignty is also limited. The sovereign cannot violate the natural rights of citizens i.e. right to life, liberty and property. He gives the right to go against the sovereign if any of these three rights are violated.

Further the **J. J. Rousseau** introduced the doctrine of popular sovereignty. The sovereignty belongs to people and can be exercised only in an assembly of whole people.

Jeremy Bentham an English thinker also claimed that sovereignty is not limited by law but was subjected to some moral limitations. According to him sovereign should justify his authority by useful legislation with the objective of promoting the greatest happiness of the greatest numbers.

Definitions:

Grotius "It is the supreme political power vested in him whose acts are not subject to any other and whose will cannot be overridden"

Blackstone "Sovereignty is supreme irresistible absolute, uncontrolled authority in which the supreme legal power resides".

Jean Bodin: Sovereignty is the "supreme power over citizens and subjects unrestrained by law".

J. W Garner: Sovereignty is "Characteristics of the state by virtue of which it cannot be legally bound except by its own will or limited by any other power than itself".

Soltaire Sovereignty is "the exercise of final legal coercive power of the state".

Willoughly Sovereignty is "the supreme will of the state"

Characteristic features of sovereignty

- **Absoluteness**: Sovereignty is regarded as absolute because it cannot be limited or restricted by a superior power or authority.
- **Permanence**: Sovereignty is permanent although in modern days it is exercised temporarily. E.g. in modern time sovereignty is held by state but exercised by the govt. Govt. comes and goes

but state always remains.

- **Universality**: Sovereignty is universal as it extends to all groups, areas, things under its jurisdiction.
- **Inalienability**: Sovereignty cannot be transferred or given away without destroying the state.
- **Individuality**: As sovereignty is an absolute power, it cannot be divided. It must be vested in a single body.

Aspects of Sovereignty: Following are some of the aspect of sovereignty.

- **Legal Sovereignty:** It is associated with supreme law making authority of State having the power to issue final command e.g. Parliament of India.
- **Political Sovereignty:** Legal sovereignty has to take into consideration the will of another authority i.e. political sovereignty. It signifies the power of electorate.
- **Titular Sovereignty:** It is that kind of sovereignty in which sovereign enjoys power only in theory but in actual practice its power is enjoyed by some other authority. E.g. President of India and King of Britain etc.
- **Actual Sovereignty:** It is that kind of sovereignty in which sovereign enjoys power in theory as well as practically e.g. President of USA & France etc.
- **De-jure Sovereignty:** A De-jure sovereign is one who occupies his office according to the well established laws and practice of the State and because of that has authority e.g. President of India.

De-facto Sovereignty: A De-facto sovereign is one who occupies highest office of the State by illegal and unconstitutional manner and makes use of force to enforce his will. E.g. General Parvez Musharaf when he was PM of Pakistan.

Austin's Theory of Sovereignty

Out of the four elements of the state Sovereignty is very crucial elements. It is the only feature which distinguishes the state from other institutions or associations in the society. John Austin was an English legal theorist. He has given the monistic concept of sovereignty. It means simply there must be a single sovereign in the state. This theory is also known as classical theory of sovereignty. His concept of sovereignty is primarily based on the concepts of Kautilya, Machiavelli, Thomas Hobbes and Jeremy Bentham. All of them advocated an unlimited sovereignty so as to control the cruelty of human being and make him a civilized citizen.

According to Austin "if a determined human superior, not in the habit of obedience to a like superior, receives habitual obedience from the bulk of given society that determined superior is sovereign in that society".

He has given his theory of sovereignty in his book 'Lecture on Jurisprudence' 1832. According to Austin, sovereignty is absolute, permanent, universal and individual. Sovereign must be a determinate authority. The determinate authority is to be found in every sovereign state.

The man who gives command himself does not obey it. The state is a legal order in which there is a determinate authority acting as the ultimate source of power. Its authority is unlimited. It may act unwisely or dishonestly but there is no limit on the exercise of its power. This theory is also known as classical or legal or monistic theory of sovereignty. Sovereignty is necessary for the state as it is one of the four elements which make a state.

There cannot be a state without sovereignty. If state is the body, sovereignty is its spirit. The state cannot alienate itself from the power of sovereignty as a human being cannot survive without his head or brain. The end of sovereignty means the end of state.

Features of Austin theory of Sovereignty:

- **Crucial element:** Sovereignty is one of the crucial elements of the four elements which make a State. There cannot be a State without sovereignty. The end of sovereignty means the end of

State. Sovereignty distinguishes the state from the other associations in the society. Just like the head of a human being cannot be separated from the body in the same sense sovereignty cannot be separated from the state.

- **Indivisible:** According to him, State is a legal order in which Sovereignty can be located very clearly. Sovereign must be a human being or a body of human being who can be identified. If it is in a body of persons it must operate in co-ordination as a single body without any division.
- **Mass Obedience:** Sovereignty receives habitual obedience from the people. If a part of the population refuses to accept him and render disobedience, he is no longer a sovereign. The loss of sovereignty leads to destruction to the institution of state.
- **Legitimacy:** Sovereignty has the legitimate physical force to extend command and obedience and enforce its laws. It is legal according to law of the land. This legitimacy makes it compulsory to all the citizens to obey the command of the sovereign.
- **Law:** Law is nothing more than the command of sovereign. He is the source of all laws in the state. He can create laws and can also amend the old ones. He can ban any illegal practice according to his will.
- **Independence:** Sovereignty is independent from internal or external control. A state no longer remains the state if its sovereignty is dominated by the external state. Both the internal as well as external dimensions of sovereignty are important for survival and growth of the state.
- **Source:** Sovereign is source of all the things good or bad in the state. His authority is absolute and unlimited.

Criticism:

This theory of sovereignty was soon criticized by the pluralistic theory of sovereignty. Since Austin's theory treat sovereignty as supreme power of State that is absolute, permanent, universal and individual. But pluralists are of the view that State is only an association in society so the sovereignty should also belong to other associations in society.Following are some of criticism made against the Austin's theory of Sovereignty.

- **Not Determinate:** As Austin claims that sovereignty is determinate but in modern world particularly in democratic countries it is not easy to determine the location of sovereignty. Every time it makes confusion weather the ruler of country is sovereign or head of country or the voters.
- **Not absolute and unlimited:** Sovereignty is absolute and unlimited according to the Austin but practically it is not true in this modern and globalized world. Sovereignty is limited by various factors which directly or indirectly affect the working of sovereignty.
- **Political Sovereignty:** Austin stresses on legal sovereignty but ignores the political sovereignty. In modern world sovereignty depends upon the political sovereignty for its functioning. Indian parliament is sovereign but it cannot go against the voters of India.
- **Against Democracy:** Austin had advocated the absolute sovereignty but in modern developed and democratic state absolute sovereignty has no space. World War 1st and World War 2nd were the results of some absolute sovereign rules of that time. In addition to it the recent war between Ukraine and Russia is also a result of the unlimited sovereignty of Putin in Russia.
- **Dangerous:** Unlimited sovereignty as advocated by Austin is against the peace of the world. In the curiosity to grab more area an unlimited sovereign ruler leads the country to the destruction of the state as well as the world. We have also seen this experience from the behaviour of Japan and Germany before and during world war 2nd.

Conclusion: Thus according to Austin, sovereignty is the supreme power of the state that is absolute, permanent, universal, inalienable, exclusive and indivisible. However, these characteristics are not acceptable to the pluralists who reject the entire thesis of Austin in total but these principles are still beneficial if we consider the negative nature of human being as predicted by Aristotle, Kautilya, Machiavelli and Thomas Hobbes.

Pluralistic Theory of Sovereignty

This theory of sovereignty is based on the concept of political pluralism. Political Pluralism refers to the doctrine that there are certain groups in the society such as family, church, union etc which were neither created by state nor authorised or approved by it. They believe that these groups help human being more than the state. On its basis the pluralistic claim that the authority should also belong to these important groups. So they believe that there must be plurality of sovereignty.

This theory was opposite to the monistic or classical theory of the sovereignty of the State. According to them Austin theory of sovereignty cannot be verified from the history. The pluralists don't believe that the sovereignty is determinate. It was possible in old days at the time of kings only.

In a federal State it becomes very difficult in present time. In federal country it is the constitution which is supposed to be sovereign but it is not a human being, hence not sovereign. They are of the view that State is only an association from many association in society hence its sovereignty cannot be unlimited.

Unlike monistic theory they believe that sovereignty is not the exclusive prerogative of the State and is shared by the various groups and associations present in the society.

The Pluralists also reject the notion of law as advocated by Austin. According to Austin, law is the command of the superior and this command is from higher to inferior. Laski termed this as ridiculous. He pointed out that to call law, as a command from the higher to the inferior, is to strain its definition to the verge of indecency. Laws are universal in character and are applied on both the lawmaker as well as the subjects. But in the case of a command, the commanding authority is over and above its command and is not bound by it.

Pluralistic theorists believe that 'state is the association of associations' which means that state is just like the other associations in the society such as family, church etc and its main function is to make co-ordination among these associations.

The doctrine of pluralism was developed by various political thinkers such as Emile Durkheim a French scholar, Otto von Gierke a German, F W Waitland an English and G D H Cole an English Economist.

Gierke and Waitland claim that law is not made by state alone but several social groups make their own contribution.

Similarly, MacIver criticised Austin's concept of law as misleading as it denies two of the basic attributes which every law exhibits- its universality and formality.

This theory of pluralistic sovereignty was advocated by J N Figgi, Paul Boncour, Maclver, Lasaki, G D H Cole and Follet. Among them Laski and Maclver are the most outstanding.

Leon Duguit a French legal philosopher claims that law is not command of an absolute sovereignty. It is the condition of social solidarity. Laws are not command of determinate human superior as claimed by Austin. They obeyed because they are crucial for the functioning of the human society. He subordinates state to the rule of social solidarity. He argued that 'public service rather than sovereignty is the essential characteristics of the state'.

Hugo Krabbe a Dutch jurist made a distinction between law and state. Law is independent and superior to the state. Sovereignty is an attribute of law and not of state.

A D Lindsay an English political thinker claims that state is only one of the numerous associations each of which possess a unique personality of its own, therefore he stressed that these associations must be given greater authority so much so that they can legislate for themselves.

Ernest Barker an English philosopher argued that state should adjust the relations of other associations to itself and between other associations in order to maintain integrity among their functioning.

He viewed state as association of associations, a community of communities for harmonizing the interest of different groups as well as individual.

As the Austin is believed to be the champion of monistic theory of sovereignty in the same sense Harold J Laski is believed to be the champion of pluralistic theory of sovereignty. He criticised the theory of state sovereignty and claimed that this theory will soon become useless as divine theory of sovereignty. He accepts Sir Henry Marine's criticism of monistic theory that it is limited by the customs and traditions. Laski says that everyone knows that to regard the King in Parliament as a sovereign body in Austinian sense is useless as no such powerful King in Parliament can ban Roman Catholic or ban trade unions.

He makes a distinction between state and government. The sovereignty in modern world lies in the Government. The Government can never be allowed to become absolute sovereign. He also believes that state is association of associations. Sovereignty in the state should be shared by many groups according to the respective value of functions of each group. In his work 'A Grammar of Politics 1938' he claimed that 'society is federal, authority must be federal also'.

According to him in the society industry and politics is controlled by the economic overlords, which is a characteristic feature of the capitalist civilization. This scenario can be transformed only instruments of production are controlled by the community. For this transformation be shifts from the Marxist solution and offers a scheme of the democratization of the power i.e. a pluralistic solution. He identified four basis of economic power i.e. supply of capital and credit, ownership and control of land, control of import and export and finally control of transport, fuel and power. Socialization of these four bases of economic power will result in decentralization of power.

Features of Pluralistic theory of Sovereignty:

- State is not the only association in society, there are various other social economic and other groups through which individual try to attain their best selves.
- These groups don't depend on State for their existence.
- Public Service rather than sovereignty is the essential characteristic of State.
- The various associations such as church and trade union etc. are same important as State and must be autonomous as State.
- Even through pluralist are not willing to regard state as absolute power but are willing to acknowledge it as a legal power.
- They consider absolute sovereignty as dangerous.
- State is neither the creator of law nor above it.
- Law came to existence long before the State came.
- They lay emphasis on the international cooperation and therefore like the State to observe the principle of international law and morality.

They attach great importance to decentralism of authority which plays an important role in Local self govt.

Multiple Choice Questions

1. Which of the following is not related to social contract theory?

a. Thomas Hobbes
b. J. J. Rousseau
c. John Locke
d. Aristotle

1. Which among the following is known as father of **utilitarianism**?

a. Karl Marx
b. Mao
c. Jeremy Bentham
d. None of the above

3. Who among the following transformed socialism into revolutionary socialism?

a. Plato
b. Karl Marx
c. John Rawls
d. None of the above

4. 'Communist Manifesto' was written by

a. Thomas Hobbes
b. Hans J. Morgenthau
c. Karl Marx
d. None of the above

5. Gandhi ji was a

a. Philosophical Anarchist
b. Revolutionary Anarchist
c. Socialist Anarchist
d. None of the above

6. According to the Plato the population of a state must be about

a. 5040
b. 6000
c. 10000
d. None of the above

7. According to the J. J. Rousseau the population of a state must be about

a. 5040
b. 6000
c. 10000

d. None of the above

8. Who wrote the book 'Lecture on Jurisprudence'?

a. Austine
b. Machiavelli
c. George Sabine
d. None of the above

9. The term 'Sovereignty' is derived from Latin word

a. Supreme
b. Superanus
c. Higher
d. None of the above

11. Who among the following was not a Marxist thinker

a. Vladimir Lenin
b. L. Trotsky
c. Antonio Gramsci
d. Gandhi Ji

10. Who said that the state of nature was a **noble savage**?

a. Thomas Hobbes
b. J. J. Rousseau
c. T. H. Green
d. None of the above

11. Which among the following article of Indian Constitution deals with definition of State?

a. Article 9
b. Article 10

c. Article 12
d. None of the above

12. Which among the following is politically a state?

a. Punjab
b. Haryana
c. Jammu and Kashmir
d. None of the above

13. Which among the following are the features of the State?

a. Population and territory
b. Government and sovereignty
c. Both a and b
d. None of the above

14. Who gave concept of **natural rights** in social contract theory?

a. Jeremy Bentham
b. J. S. Mill
c. John Locke
d. None of the above

15. Who wrote **Leviathan**

a. T. H Green
b. Thomas Hobbes
c. Karl Marx
d. None of the above

16. The concept of **general will** was given by

a. J. J. Rousseau
b. M. K. Gandhi

c. Subash Chander Bose
d. None of the above

17. Who gave a concept of **absolute sovereignty** in social contract theory?

a. Thomas Hobbes
b. J. S. Mill
c. T. H. Green
d. None of the above

18. Who said 'state is the march of god on earth'?

a. Karl Marx
b. Jeremy Bentham
c. Georg Wilhelm Friedrich Hegel
d. None of the above

19. American and French revolutions were inspired by

a. Thomas Hobbes
b. John Locke
c. Machiavelli
d. None of the above

Answer Key
1. (d) 2. (c) 3. (b) 4. (c) 5. (a) 6. (a)
7. (c) 8. (a) 9. (b) 10. (d) 11. (b) 12. (c)
13. (d) 14. (c) 15. (c) 16. (b) 17. (a) 18. (a)
19. (c) 20. (b)

Exercise for Practice

Short answer type questions

Q1. Define State and discuss its elements?
Q2. 'State is March of God on earth' Comment?
Q3. Define Society? Distinguish between State and Society?

Q4. Define State? Differentiate between State and Nation?

Q5. Define State? Differentiate between State and Society?

Q6. Define between Nation and Society?

Q7. Define State? Discuss its Evolutionary theory of origin of state?

Q8. Discuss social contract theory?

Q9. Write a note on social contract theory as given by Hobbes?

Q10. Write a note on social contract theory as given by John Locke?

Q11. Write a note on social contract theory as given by J. J. Rousseau?

Q12. Define Divine theory of origin of state?

Q13. Discuss the organic theory of Nature of the state?

Q14. Discuss the Marxist theory of nature of State?

Q15. Define Sovereignty? Discuss its location in democracy?

Q16. Explain in brief the Austin Theory of Sovereignty?

Q17. Explain in brief the Pluralist Theory of Sovereignty?

Long Answer type question

Q1. Explain in detail the Social contract theory with special reference to Hobbes, Locke and Rousseau?

Q2. Define the state and explain its elements?

Q3. Define the term State? Differentiate between State, Society and Nation?

Q3. Define Sovereignty? Discuss the Pluralistic theory of sovereignty?

Q4. Define Sovereignty? Discuss the Austin theory of sovereignty?

or

Q. Define Sovereignty? Discuss the Monistic theory of sovereignty?

CHAPTER THREE

BASIC CONCEPTS

Equality and Proportionate Equality

Equality: It is the same treatment in case of punishment as well as reward and granting rights etc. without any discrimination on basis of class, caste, colour, creed, place of birth and sex etc. Equality is mostly granted by an authority usually by the state. A democratic state gives more equality to its citizens as compared to communist and absolute monarchy. God has not created the entire human being equal on this earth, so absolute equality is not possible.

The notion of equality too emerged in Greek philosophy. There were two groups one of Plato and Aristotle advocating inequality. The other consisting of Pericles, The Sophists, Antiphon, Lycophron, Eurpises and Stoics advocating equality among man. During the medieval, Christianity too advocated inequality by the notion that in the eyes of God all were equal but there are inequalities on earth. The Renaissance and the Reformation played an important part in weakening this unequal social and political system. The Glorious revolution of 1688 in England, The American Deceleration of Independence of 1776, and the French Revolution of 1789 helped the cause of equality.

Definitions

According to international Encyclopaedias of Social Sciences "Equality refers sometimes to certain properties which men are held to have in common but more often to certain treatments which men either receive or ought to receive".

Barker "Equality after all is a derivative value, it is derived from the supreme value of development of personality"

Harrington: "Equality of estates caused equality of power and equality of power is liberty"

J. F. Stephen "Equality is a word as wide and vague as to be by itself almost unmeaning"

J. R. Lucas "Equality before law does not guarantee equal treatment by the law but equal excess to the law and consideration only only of those factors laid down by the law as relevant"

Lord Action "The passion for equality makes vain the hope of freedom"

Louis Blanc "An ideal condition of socio-economic equality is expressed from each according to his ability to each according to his need".

Plato "All men are by nature equal, made of same earth and by one workman and however we deceive ourselves as dear unto God as the poor peasant as the mighty prince".

Kinds of Equality

Since equality is a multidimensional concept it has different kinds as shown below;

- **Natural Equality**: It is based on the notion that all human being are created equally by God with equal talent. It directs the state to reduce inequality in the society by proving opportunity to all. This kind of equality is idealistic. It is believed that all human phenomena including death, birth and body structure was created by a super power called God. If we follow this argument the destiny of birth, your body structure and the incidental death are some of the inequalities by God.
- **Political Equality**: It is based on the notion that all the human being should have the right to contest and vote in election. It criticizes any discrimination based on sex and colour etc. in case of voting right. To achieve it the state provides various rights to the citizens. It is a peculiar feature of the democracy. In democracy citizen are supposed to be equal as compared to

the citizens in the un-democratic countries. In simple words granting equality to all the citizens in the political activities including voting in election, contesting elections for political offices etc. is called political equality.

- **Social Equality**: It is based on the notion that every citizen has equal access to various opportunities in the society. This concept is a difficult to attain by a society. Everybody has the right to have an equal dignity in the society because a human being is an important part of the society. This social equality is believed to be achieved more in the socialist countries. The contemporary situation of the world shows that this is also achieved in the democratic countries.
- **Economic Equality**: It is based on the notion that there should not be the concentration of economic power in the hand of few elite. It advocates the policy of taxation so as to reduce gap between rich and poor. Although it is very difficult for any state to achieve the complete economic equality still with the taxation we can reduce the gap between the rich and the poor in the state. Socialist thinkers have criticised the capitalist system for the formation of economic inequality. In actual practice the socialist were also failed to provide a proper economic equality to their citizens. The state should adjust the means of production and distribution in such a manner that no citizen can become so rich to purchase a poor citizen and a poor citizen can never become so poor to sell himself.
- **Legal Equality**: It is based on the notion that all the human beings are equal before law. Law is supreme and no one is above law. This equality is too followed in the democratic countries which treat the law above all.
- **International Equality**: It is based on the notion that all the nations are equal in international sphere despite their size, economic condition, geographical or militarily composition. E.g. United Nation holds that all nations are equal.

Different thinkers have suggested different solution to achieve equality. The liberal thinkers suggest the liberty and capitalism as the way for equality. They believe that equality can be achieved only in a democratic country. Anarchist thinkers believe in the abolition of state for establishment of equality. Marxist thinkers also suggest the abolition of state and establishment of classless society for the establishment of equality but in a different pattern as claimed by Anarchist thinkers.

Proportionate equality: It believes that equality should not be applied forcefully but there should be a rational justification for it. The goods should be distributed according to the merit of the citizens. In democratic country there is proportionate equality. The government also takes care of the poor and backward section of the people by applying welfare policies for their survival and development.

Proportionate equality is not a new term. It was also present during the the days of Plato and Aristotle in Ancient Greece. Aristotle identified distributive justice with 'proportionate equality' i.e. the view that goods should be distributed not strictly equally as in arithmetic justice but in proportion to their worth or merit.

According to Karl Marx the distribution of the goods must be according to the principle 'from each according to the ability to each according to his need' whereas Lenin, a Russian Marxist modified it as 'from each according to ability to all according to the work'. This modified principle is today applied in the largest communist countries such as Russia and China.

In India too this principle is applied. We provide different salaries to different employees depending upon their nature of contribution i.e. work. We also have the various welfare schemes for the welfare of the poor section of the people.

Two terms are important in the domain of equality i.e. equality before law and equal protection of law. Equality before law states that all persons are equal in the eyes of law and there will no discrimination with respect to law on any issue. Equal protection of law says that although all the persons are equal before law but if law feels that it is necessary to give some concession to some people, state can discriminate positively such as government is providing reservation to the depressed classes such as ST, SC and OBC in India. Government is also giving welfare policies and free legal aid etc. to the needy people and it also comes under equal protection of law.

Liberty

Introduction

Liberty is the equality of man. Liberty simply means freedom of human being from religious, political and economic restrains. Some associate it with individualism where as others with democracy. Liberty provides an opportunity to the individuals to live their life happily.

Meaning

The word 'Liberty' is derived from Latin word Liber which means 'free'. So liberty means freedom from the restrictions imposed by state. It is a product of western countries and is popular in democratic countries. During the time of Socrates and Plato, notion of individual liberty was not advocated by thinkers. This is why Socrates does not run away from prison and accepted his death sentence.

During the medieval period, there was no idea of liberty of the individual. Divine law prevailed above human liberty. At the end of the medieval period renaissance movement emphasized the freedom of conscience.

In modern period Renaissance demanded a multi-dimension liberty. Religious liberty was demanded against the Church and the Papacy.

Economic liberty was demanded against feudal economic order. Political liberty was demanded against the monarchs. Liberty leads to a broad stream of ideology known as liberalism.

Early exponents of liberalism include John Locke (1632-1704), Adam Smith (1723-90) and Jeremy Bentham (1748-1832). Locke is known as the father of liberalism, Smith is known as the father of economics and political economy and Bentham as the founder of utilitarianism. All of them defended the principle of laissez-faire which implies the least interference of the state in the economic activities of individuals. They are the founders of Classical Liberalism which is also called negative liberalism because it envisions a negative role of the state in the sphere of mutual interaction of individuals.

Locke emphasized toleration and freedom of individual conscience. Bentham emphasized the expansion of the market economy and restriction of the sphere of state activity. Mill sought to revise this view of utilitarian to plead for the expansion of state activity for the promotion of general welfare. He recommended positive role of the state for the promotion of individual liberty.

Definitions

T H. Green “Liberty is the positive power of doing and enjoying those things which are worthy of doing and enjoying”

Seeley “Liberty is the opposite of over-government”

Laski “Liberty is the eager maintenance of that atmosphere in which men have opportunity to be their best selves”.

G D H Cole “Liberty is the freedom of the individual to express without external hindrances to personality”.

Columbia Encyclopaedia “Liberty is a word used to describe various types of individual freedom such as religious liberty, political liberty, freedom of speech, right of self-defence and the like”.

Berlin “Negative liberty of the individual consists in not being prevented from attaining his goal by other human beings”

Berlin “Positive liberty does not interpret freedom as simply being left alone but as self mastery”

J J Rousseau: “Liberty consists in obedience to General Will”.

J. S. Mill view on Liberty: Mill begins his earlier thought about liberty as a champion of classical liberalism. He agreed with his teacher Bentham that every action of the state should be judged by the principle of greatest happiness of greatest number. Liberty in a state can be achieved if the state follows the principle of greatest happiness of greatest number.

With the development of his independent thought like Aristotle he too criticises his teacher Bentham on the issue that his teacher is wrong on this principle as he is concentrating on quantity not on the quality of happiness. He then makes making a difference between quality and quantity of happiness by saying that it is better to be a human being dissatisfied than a pig satisfied, better to be **Socrates** dissatisfied than a fool satisfied.

Mill in his essay '**On Liberty**' (1859) sought to demonstrate the danger to which individual liberty was exposed in a democracy. While Bentham and James Mill believe that democratic government could act for good of the whole of society J. S. Mill thought that democratic rule was synonymous with majority rule and that majorities may tend to oppress minorities. In this case he was inspired by the view expressed by Alexis de Tocqueville a French Philosopher in his celebrated work '**Democracy in America**'.

Mill defends Liberty of individual to ensure fullest development of his personality. He identified three major areas in which liberty of individual must be protected. While he advocates fullest liberty in the sphere of thought and expression while some restrictions in the sphere of freedom of action and freedom of association.

He classified the action of individual into two types i.e. self regarding actions and other regarding actions. Self regarding actions are those which affects only self whereas other regarding actions are those which affect others. He recommends complete freedom in self regarding actions while some restriction in other regarding actions. The state could also interfere in the self regarding actions if it was thought to be particularly injurious to individual himself. He clearly mentions that the only purpose for which power can be rightfully exercised over any members of a civilized community, against his will, is to prevent harm to others. Mill argued that liberty and democracy, taken together create the possibility of human excellence.

T. H. Green view on Liberty:

He was an English philosopher born at Yorkshine in England in 1836. He was educated at Balliol College Oxford where he became a professor of Moral Philosophy in 1878. He is popular for adding the moral dimension to the philosophy of Liberalism.

He sought to add a moral dimension to concept of liberty and thus advanced a full-fledged theory of the welfare state. He was deeply influenced by the idealist tradition which originated from the writings of Plato, Aristotle and other idealistic thinkers.

Green is hailed as the architect of the modern welfare state. He viewed that we must all probably agree that freedom, rightly understood is the greatest of blessings that its attainment is the true end of all our effort as citizens. When we thus speak of freedom we should consider carefully what we mean by it. We do not mean merely freedom from restraint or compulsion. We do not mean a freedom that can be enjoyed by one man or one set of men as the cost of a loss of freedom to others.

According to Green "human consciousness postulates liberty, liberty involves rights and right demand the state". He treats state as an instrument for the perfection of the individual. State should create social, economic and political environment in which individual will have the best chance of acting according to their conscience.

Green saw society not as a collection of self interested individuals as suggested by social contractual theorist or utilitarian theorist but as a structure of traditions, laws and institutions that unite individuals into a larger ethical whole. It is this structure of tradition that constitutes the moral progress of mankind. He wanted to make a connection between action of individual and morality. Unless there is a positive connection between our actions and some moral purposes, we cannot truly be said to be free.

Human being doesn't seek pleasure directly. Rational basis of human activity is will and reason and not desire and passion. Men therefore seek self realization which is superior to all sort of pleasure. He treats human being as self conscious subjects and pursues their good but their good doesn't vary from person to person as claimed by classical liberals.

T.H Green said that the true liberty or positive freedom of man consists in the act of "Good Will" it is a positive power of doing or enjoying something worth doing or enjoying and that too, something that we do or enjoy in common with others. It is more than the mere absence of impediment to our desires. The freedom to be genuine, one should be provided with full opportunity other than the interference of others. He set out a number of different descriptions of the positive concept of freedom.

Types of Liberty: Broadly speaking liberty is of two types i.e. Negative Liberty and Positive Liberty.

There are two concept of liberty i.e. Negative Liberty and Positive Liberty.

Negative Liberty

- It begins with the industrial revolution of 17th century in Europe.
- Negative Liberty highlights the negative role of state.
- They advocate the absence of all restrains by state.
- They support a minimal state.
- They oppose that state's role in imposing its own conception of good on the individuals in their mutual dealings.
- They believe that state is a necessary evil.
- They treat individual as social rational being, who knows his good and bad, so they avoid interference of state in their life.
- They believe that everyone knows his own interest best and that state should not decide his end and purposes.
- Some advocates of negative liberty are Adam Smith, Jeremy Bentham, James Mill, Henry Sedgwick, Isaiah Berlin and Spencer.

Positive Liberty:

- The concept of positive liberty developed during the latter half of the nineteenth century.
- It advocates positive role of state.

- It promotes the state to provide welfare policies in order to change from police state to welfare state.
- Macpherson calls it as 'developmental liberty'.
- It advocates the taxation of rich by state for the welfare of the poor.
- It promotes welfare policies for the poor classes such as ST/SC/OBC/Women to reduce rich poor gap.
- Rousseau, Kant, Hegel, Green, Barker, Laski, Macpherson etc. are some of the advocates of positive liberty.

Relationship between liberty and equality

- Liberty and equality are essential for social justice.
- During the American and French revolution slogans of Liberty, equality and Fraternity were raised.
- Some writers such as Lord Action, Alexis De Tocqueville, Friedman and Hayek are of the view that liberty and equality are incompatible with each other.
- Some of the writers such as Laski, Barker, Tawney and Maitland are of the view that liberty and equality are compatible with each other.
- In Democratic state an, individual need both liberty and equality.
- According to A F Pollard, liberty lies in equality.

Capitalism is helpful for liberty but equality and capitalism are opposite.

Right and various Perspectives (Liberal and Marxist)

Right

Right are simply the claims which help the individuals to attain their best selves so as to develop them. Rights are recognized and sanctioned by society. There cannot be right outside society. Democratic countries are supposed to provide more right to their citizens than communist and absolute monarch countries.

Definitions:

Bosanquet "A right is a claim recognized by society and enforced by state"

Plamentaz "Rights must have a foundation of right as against wrong"

Green "Rights represent an attainable ideal which the state seeks to achieve"

Baker "Right are the external conditions necessarily for the greatest possible development of the capacities of the personality".

Laski "Rights are those condition of social life without which no man can seek, in general to be his best self".

Laski "Every state is known by the rights it maintains".

Wilde "Rights are reasonable claims to freedom in exercise of certain activities".

Bentham "Rights, properly so called, are the creatures of law properly so called real laws give birth to real rights"

Beni Prasad "Rights are nothing more and nothing less than those social conditions which are necessary or favourable to development of personality".

Characteristics of rights:

- Rights are guaranteed by State.
- Rights are protected by govt.
- Rights are prior to State.
- Right have a pre-political character.
- The State doesn't create right, it only recognizes them.
- Rights belong to individual & not to state.
- Rights are the condition of good life.
- Rights are dynamic as they change with time and circumstances.
- They are not absolute and are having some restrictions.
- Rights have a moral character.
- Rights in a country changes depending upon the system of govt. i.e. democratic, monarchy, capitalist, communist etc.
- Rights are closely associated with duties.

Liberal Prospective of Rights:

This theory of right stresses on the welfare of the individuals. It postulates that right are, in essence, conditions of social welfare. The State should set out all other considers and recognizes only such rights as are designed to promote social welfare. Various theories have been developed such as theory of natural rights as given by Pain and T. H. Green, theory of legal right by Hobbes and Bentham etc. The Utilitarian school of ninetieth century, led by Bentham, postulated the 'greatest happiness of greatest number' as the sole criterion of legislation and recognition of rights. Liberals view rights mainly in three types i.e. Natural Rights, Moral Rights and Legal Rights.

- **Natural Rights**: These are those rights which are enjoyed by human being because they are human being. These rights are supposed to be blessed by God. The concept of natural rights was first of all given by Locke. According to him Rights to life, Right to Liberty and Right to property belong to Natural rights and no govt. can forbid them to its citizens.
- **Moral Rights**: these are those rights which have moral bases. These are based on human sense of goodness and justice. These are not assisted by the force of law. There are no sanctions on violation of moral rights as for legal rights.
- **Legal Rights**: these are those rights which are accepted and enforced by the state. Any defaulter of legal right gets a punishment in its return. They are maintained by the state to make law and order in order to distinguish it from the state of nature i.e. lawlessness.

Marxist Prospective of Rights:

The Marxist theory of right can be understood in terms of the economic system at a particular period of history. The State is being an instrument in the hand of economically dominant class and the law it forms is also a class law. In feudal State, through feudal laws protect the system of right favouring the feudal system. In the capitalist State, through the capitalist laws, protects the system of right favouring the capital system.

According to Marx, the class which controls the economic structure of the society also controls political power and it uses this power to protect and promote its interest than the interest of all. In the socialist society, through the proletarian laws, would protect and promote the interest/rights of the working class but it will promote the interest of all because there will be compulsory physical labour. As the socialist society unlike capitalist society is a classless society so it will protect and promote the interest of all. Marx was of the view that socialist state would seek to establish socialism which will be based on the principle of 'from all according to his ability to each according to his work'.

Features of Marx concept of Justice:

a. **Division of society:** According to Marx at every stages of history the state is divided into two sections i.e. haves and haven't. Haves control the means of production whereas haven't don't have such control. This division in the distribution of power leads to revolution which brings change in system.
b. **Importance of workers:** In his writing '**Communist manifesto**' he makes a call to the workers of the world to unite and fight against this capitalist system. He appreciates them that they have nothing to lose except the chains in their hands and they have a world to win.
c. **Surplus value:** The difference between manufacturing price including labour and raw material cost and selling price is called surplus value. Instead of spending on the welfare of worker class, it is kept by the capitalist class without disclosing its value to the workers.
d. **Means of production:** Those who controls the means of production also controls the political power. He motivates the workers to capture the means of productions and rest system such as political system and religion etc. will be changed automatically.

e. **Dictatorship of proletariat:** It will be a transitional phase between the capitalist stage and socialist stage. During this stage the workers will be in power. They will destroy each and every thing of capitalist state and help to achieve the classless society.
f. **Stateless society:** He believes in the classless and stateless society so that every person will have to work physically. The state will work on the principle of 'from each according to each according to his need'.
g. **Revolution:** Karl Marx was in favour of a peaceful transition form a capitalist state to a socialist state. He was of the view that the capitalist will not agree for a peaceful transition. So the workers had to do a revolution violent if needed to establish the socialist system.

Democracy: Meaning, Evolution and Types

Democracy

The word Democracy has been derived from two Greek words i.e. 'Demos' which means the people and 'Kratos' which means 'rule' or 'government'. Thus 'democracy' means 'the rule of the people'. Democracy is that form of government in which the real authority of government lies in the ordinary people so that their interest can be served better.

Democracy has been described as one of the characteristic institution of modernity and as such it was the result of a complex and intertwined process of ideological, social and economic change.

In Britain, this change was signalled by the Industrial Revolution that began in the middle of the eighteenth century, while in France and America it was launched by the political revolutions in the last quarter of the same century. Britain is regarded as the first modern democracy because, in the aftermath of the Civil War in the seventeenth century. Royal absolute was brought to an end and powers were transferred from the crown to the two houses of parliament, of which one, the House of Commons, was an elected chamber.

Definitions

Abraham Lincoln "Democracy is the government of the people, by the people, and for the people".

Cleon "That shall be democratic which shall be of the people, by the people, for the people".

J S Mill defined democracy as the Government in which "the whole people or some numerous portions of them exercise the governing power through deputies periodically elected by them".

John Seeley defines Democracy as "a government in which everyone has a share".

Hall "Democracy is that form of political organization in which public opinion has control".

C B Macpherson "Democracy is merely a mechanism for choosing and authorizing government or in some other way getting laws and political decision made".

Dicey "Democracy is the form of government in which the governing body is a comparatively large fraction of the entire nation".

Gettell "Democracy is that form of government in which the mass of the population possesses the right to share in the exercise of sovereign power".

Lowell "In a democracy no one can complain that he has not a chance to be heard"

Sartoori "Democracy is a procedure in which leaders compete at elections for authority to govern"

Evolution

Beginning from the ancient Greek to present day Europe, democracy has changed from its old concept to the modern concept of democracy i.e. liberal democracy. Democracy began its journey from the ancient Greek particularly in Athens and Sparta. Democracy at that time was not democracy in actual sense, as all the persons living were not given citizenship. Although there was direct democracy but those having citizenship could only take part in affair of state. It was so bad that Plato, the father of political philosophy called democracy as the rule of ignorant. Aristotle too criticized it as a corrupt form of govt.

Britain is regarded as the first modern democracy because after the civil war of 17th century, royal absolutism was brought to an end and power was transferred to the two houses of parliament. In France democracy arrived, after the revolution of 1789 with its slogan Liberty, Equality and Fraternity with the declaration of the Right of Man and Citizens. In United States of America, democracy began with the American Revolution having the slogan of 'no tax without representation'. The political idea of John Lock, Tom Paine and documents like the 'French Declaration of the Rights of Man (1789), American Declaration of Independence (1776) expressed important idea of Democracy.

With the 1st world war democracy was criticized and with the emergence of ideologies such as Nazism in Germany and Fascism in Italy, it was criticized. Karl Marx gave concept of scientific socialism to avoid evil effect of democracy and divided the world into two blocks but with the collapse of USSR, democracy is supposed to be superior and the world now a day have no alternate for it.

Types of Democracy

Broadly classified there are two types of democracy i.e. direct democracy and indirect democracy. Direct democracy is again divided into Referendum, Initiative, Plebiscite and Recall.

Direct Democracy: It is that system in which the people directly participate in the governance. In such a system all the citizens are involved in the functioning of govt. In ancient times it was in the city-states of Rome and Greece. Today also it is found in Switzerland both at federal and local level. Some of devices of direct democracy are;

- **Referendum**: Under this people have the power to finally determine the fate of legislative measure passed by the legislation.
- **Initiative**: It refers to the right of the people to propose measure for legislation before the legislature.

- **Plebiscite**: It means the system of eliciting public opinion/ decision on any issue or problem being faced by the government.
- **Recall**: It gives the people the right to call back their elected representatives in case they are not satisfied with their work.

Indirect Democracy: It is also known as representative democracy. In large country direct democracy is not possible so an alternative to direct democracy is representative democracy. Indirect democracy can be called an updated or modified version of direct democracy. In this type of democracy the people elect their representatives for a fixed period of time and in return these representative works in process of government on the name of people for that fixed time. In modern time it is at practice in large democratic countries such as India, Pakistan and USA etc.

Concept of Justice

The word 'justice' is derived from the Latin words 'Jungere' and 'Jus'. The 'Jungere' means to bind or to tie together and 'Jus' means a bond or tie. As a bonding or joining idea, justice serves to organize people together into a fair relationship by distributing each person his due share of right and duties, rewards and punishment etc. The earliest concept of justice in Greek thought to be found in the writing of the early Pythagoreans.

Different thinkers from the time of Plato to today tried their best to provide a perfect kind of justice in society. Ernest Barker dwells on the concept of legal justice i.e. law according to justice. He draws a distinction between positive law and natural law as both derive their validity from different sources. Positive law is derived and declared by each community for its members where as natural law is a universal law.

Definitions

Plato "Justice as one person, one duty, one class and one work".

Aristotle "Justice as proportionate equality".

Thomas Hobbes "Justice consists in working according to law"

John Lock "Justice is a bond which holds the society together".

Mark "Justice is achieved with the elimination of class society and establishment of classless society".

C. E. Marriam "Justice consists in a system of understandings and procedure through which each is agreed upon as fair"

John Rawls "Justice as fairness"

Liberal perspective of justice: Liberal treats liberty of the individual as the necessary condition for justice in the society. They treat state as important institution for the welfare of human being. Classical liberal thinkers advocated a limitation on the authority of the state so that individual could get justice. They limit the state for security and other few things. They had advocated a negative role of the state in the development of human being. Modern liberal treats state as important institution for the welfare of individual. They advocate the positive role of the state for the growth, welfare and justice in the society.

Liberal thinkers believe that justice can be achieved only in a democratic state. They are against socialism.

John Rawls an American thinker in his work 'A Theory Justice' has pointed out that a good society is characterised by a number of virtues. Justice is the first virtue of a good society. In a just society, justice is established as the foundation of social structure. Hence all political and legislative decisions should be designed to fulfil the requirements of justice.

According to Rawls, the problem of justice consists in ensuring a just distribution of 'primary goods' which includes rights and liberties, powers and opportunities, income and wealth, means of self respect etc. He criticised Bentham and his principle of greatest happiness of greatness number.

Immanuel Kant believed that if justice and righteousness perish, human life would no longer have any value in the world.

Marxist perspective of Justice: Marxist thinker believes that justice will be established in only after the over throw of the state and establishment of the stateless society. They believe that this system of state is established and adjusted by the bourgeois class for the domination of the working class. As long as the state exists there are no chances of getting justice.

Karl Marx and Engels in communist manifesto made calls to all the workers of the world to unite to over overthrow this system of capitalism and establishment of a class less society. They gave a call to all the workers of the world to unite as they have nothing to lose except the chains in their hand and they have a world to win. This call has inspired many minds which resulted into Russian as well as Chinese revolution.

In capitalist system workers have no real freedom as they are reduced to the need of the machines. He has no freedom to decide what he will produce. Moreover he calls for placing the control of the economic means of production under workers and over through the capitalist class.

Following are some of the characteristics of Marxist perspective on justice;

- It favours worker and advocates their welfare.
- It is against capitalist system.
- It advocates the over throw the state.
- It advocates classless society
- It is impossible to get justice in this capitalist state.
- Its origin is in the teaching of German thinker Karl Marx.
- It restricts freedom as compared to democracy.
- It claims that in communist system individual will work according to his ability and he will get according to his need.
- It is based on the analysis of history.
- Marxist socialism is the scientific form of socialism.
- It is based on compulsory physical work. It is based on the principle 'he who does not work, neither shall eat'.
- It places more stress on controlling economic means of production than political.

Dimensions of Justice:

With the development in the entire sphere of human being, the concept of justice has also changed. With the spread of democracy, and change in the function of state, from a police state to a welfare state, the concept of justice has also changed. In the ancient time what the ruler decided is supposed to be justice in that country but this notion has changed and today justice is based on reasoning of human being.

Social Justice

- It is the offspring of political justice.
- Social justice in a society implies that there are means available for social opportunities for the development of personality for the people.
- It also involves a logical synthesis of liberty, equality and fraternity.
- It also implies that people in the society should not be discriminated on the basis of caste, class and sex etc.
- In modern welfare state some positive discrimination is done to uplift the poor and depressed section of the society i.e. ST/SC/OBC/Women etc.
- The social habits and social institutions play a vital role in its implementation.

Economic Justice

- For economic justice, principle of equal pay for equal work should be prevailed.
- There cannot be social justice or political justice without economic justice.
- Economic justice means the basic need of all the member of community must be met.
- National economy should be planned so as to reduce a gap between rich and poor.
- Liberals are of the view that economic justice means to fulfil the basic need of all the human being in society.
- Marxist is of the view that economic justice is achieved only after abolition of private property.

Political Justice

- Political Justice means every adult citizen should have access to vote and contest elections.
- It also involves granting of some fundamental right to the citizens i.e. right to freedom of speech and expression and right to form association etc.
- Political Justice is possible in a democratic state.
- It involves granting of liberty, equality and fraternity to citizens.
- In political just society, the source of political power is people.
- Political justice is achieved if three organs of govt. i.e. legislative, executive and judiciary work properly.

Legal Justice: The legal dimension of justice has been emphasized by the writers of the analytical school such as John Lock, Austin and Hobbes etc. They treat law as an important instrument of justice. Each individual is entitled to the protection and the violation of law is punished in according to law. In order to have legal justice, laws are made and implemented by proper agencies such as legislative bodies.

- Legal justice demands that equal right should be made available to all the members without discrimination.
- The legal dimensions of justice are determined by the constitution as well as by the statues of the legislature.
- Legal justice demand punishment to the offenders of law.
- The implementation agency must be courts or semi judicial bodies.
- Legal justice varies from state to state. An act just in one state may be injustice in another state.
- For proper legal justice, judicial process should be simple and not very costly.
- Judiciary should be independent and impartial.

Power, Authority and Legitimacy

Power

The English word power derives from certain Latin and French word which means 'to be able'. Power is normally understood as the possession of control, authority, or influence over others, a relationship in which an individual or a group is able to exert influence over the mind and actions of other. The significance of power in political phenomenon was brought out by thinkers like Machiavelli, Hobbes, Nietzche, Max Weber, Catlin, Lasswell, Kaplan and Morgenthau.

Definitions

Arnold Woofers defines it as "to move others or to get them to do what one wants them to do and not to do, what one does not want them to do".

M G Smith says that "power is the ability to act effectively over people and things using means ranging from persuasion to coercion".

Kaplan and Lasswell defines power as "Participation in decision making".

David Easton defines it as "relationship in which one person or a group is able to determine the actions of another in the direction of the former's own ends".

Michael Foucault defines it as "Power is omnipotent; it has a transformation character, it is aligned with knowledge".

Mao "Power flows from the barrel of a gun".

Edward Shrills "Power is ability to influence the behaviour of others in accordance with one's own ends".

Characteristics of power

- It is the ability to influence the behaviour of other.
- It is not static and changes with time and situation.
- It is not absolute.
- When power is based on legitimacy, it becomes authority.
- It clearly depends on its use.

Dimension of Power

Mainly there are three dimension of power i.e.

- Political Power
- Economic Power
- Ideological Power

Political Power:

- The concept of political power is a key concept in the study of political science.
- Various thinkers such as Machiavelli, Hobbes, Montesquieu have been recognized the importance of political power in the state.
- Political power plays an important role in development of a nation.
- It is the primary step for becoming an economic powerful country.
- There are three organs of political power i.e. Legislative, Executive and Judiciary.
- Its bases are psychological influence, leadership and its will power.
- Power in a state may be centralized as in case of Britain or China or it may be decentralized as in case of USA and India.
- The centralization of power is known as unitary system in which power is held by unitary govt.
- The decentralization of power is known as federal country in which power is divided between central and state govt.

Economic Power

- Economic power is also important for a state. It is closely related to political power.
- In modern days, the power of a nation depends upon its army and weapons, which all need more and more money.

- Economic power determines the importance of the state in international relations.
- It was also supposed to be very important during the days of kings.
- It is so important that weakening of economic system was the main cause of disintegration of USSR.
- It is also the important factor beyond achieving the political power

Ideological Power

- It provides legitimacy to the ruling classes and helps them maintain their stronghold on political power.
- It has negative effect too as westernization in India is a result of Ideological power.
- Ideological Power is very important to gain political power. Nerindra Damodardas Modi, the PM of India is its live example.
- Most of political parties have their ideology fixed in advance so as to gain majority vote in election.
- Ideological power is so powerful that communism and capitalism two ideologies divided the world into two camps i.e. USSR & USA. More today's USA-North Korea conflict is also result of this ideological conflict.

Authority

The word authority was derived from the old Roman word "Auctor" or "Auctoritors" which generally means counsel or advice. It was the roman custom to get the senate made up of "men of reason" or "Elders with experience" to approve or reject the decision of the popular assembly. It is related with power. Authority is rarely exercised in the absence of power, and power always implies some amount of authority.

Definitions

Maclver "Authority is often defined as being power, the power to command obedience"

Herbert A Simmon Authority is "the power to make decisions which guide the action of others."

Jouvenel "Authority is ability of man to get his proposal accepted".

Carl Friedrich "An authority is the embodiment of reason and depends on the capacity of reasoned elaboration. The man who possesses authority has the capacity for reasoned elaboration".

Lock "People are the source of all authority".

Characteristics of Authority

Following are some of characteristics of Authority:

- It is broadly understood as a constitutional means through which one can command compliance or obedience and influence the behaviour of another.
- It has moral dimension.
- It is based on reason.
- It has responsibility for accountability.
- It is divine authority if supposed to derive from God.
- It is informal.
- It is possessed by an elite class.

Sources of Authority

According to Sociologist Max Weber, there are three sources of political authority i.e. Traditional, Charismatic and Legal Rational. They are explained in detail below.

- **Traditional Authority:** When a sovereign person holds his position due to established custom and tradition, than it is known as traditional authority. It was associated with hereditary system of power and privilege. Kings in the ancient time is its best example.
- **Charismatic Authority:** when a sovereign person hold position due to the individual's charisma or personality, than it is known

as charismatic authority. This type of authority may be 'manufactured' through the media and the 'cult of personality'. The charismatic leader has the gift of divine grace and extraordinary qualities. Narinder Modi. Gandhi, Lenin, Mao etc. are its examples.

- **Legal Rational Authority:** This form of authority is very significant in modern industrial society and is often regarded as the symbol of large-scale bureaucratic organizations and it operates through a body of clearly defined rule and procedure. Bureaucracy is its best example.

Legitimacy

The term "legitimacy" is derived from the Latin word "Legtimus" this means lawful. Legitimacy amounts to pronouncing what is lawful i.e. what is according with established rules, principles or standards. It is the power of the state rightfully exercised and is the acceptance so by those on whom it exercises its control.

Definitions

S M Lipset "Legitimacy involves the capacity of system to engender and maintain the belief that the existing political institutions are most appropriate for the society".

Robert Dahl "According to one use of term, a govt. is said to be legitimate if the people to whom its orders are directed believed that the structure, procedure, acts, decision, policies, officials or the leaders of the government passes the quality of righteousness, propriety or moral goodness and should be accepted because of this quality irrespective of the specified content of the particular act in question".

J C Plano and R E Riggs "Legitimacy means the quality of being justified or willingly accepted by subordinates that convert the exercise of political power into rightful authority".

Jean Blondel "Legitimacy can be defined as the extent to which the population accepts naturally without questioning, the organization to which it belongs".

G K Robert "Legitimacy is that principle which indicate the acceptance on the part of public of the occupancy of a political office by a particular person, or the exercise of power by a person or group, either generally or a specific instance, on the grounds that occupancy or exercise of power is in according with some generally accepted principles and procedures of enforcement of authority".

Basic of Legitimacy

Robert Dahl has given three basis of legitimacy i.e Personal Choice, Competence and Economy.

Max Weber has given three basic of legitimacy i.e. Traditional, Charismatic and Legal.

David Easton divided legitimacy into three types as given below

- **Ideological Legitimacy:** It is based on the moral convictions about the validity of the incumbents of authority. Different ideologies are used to legitimate the ruler of the country e.g. Fascism, communism and liberalism etc.
- **Structure Legitimacy:** It is based an independent belief in the validity of the structure and norms and the incumbents of the authority.
- **Personal Legitimacy:** The belief in the authority is based on their personal qualities.

Relation between authority and legitimacy;

There is a close relationship between authority and legitimacy. Legitimacy is the lawfulness of authority, and as we known only legitimate power is called authority. So authority is not possible without legitimacy. Legitimacy provides an element of willingness, on the part of people to accept the government's power to rule people. Authority possesses the power because legitimacy authorizes it to exercise power. It is the meeting point between state and the people, between the rulers and ruled. Without legitimacy there would not be an effective social order if the authority is exercised without legitimacy.

Multiple Choice Questions

1. Which of the following part of Indian Constitution deals with Rights

a. Part I
b. Part II
c. Part III
d. Part IV

2. Articles in Indian Constitution from Art 12 to Art 35 deals with

a. Directive Principles of State Policy
b. Citizenship Law
c. Emergency Provisions
d. Fundamental Rights

3. Art 51A of Indian Constitution deals with

a. Fundamental duties
b. Fundamental Rights
c. Both a and b
d. None of the above

4. Right to property in India is a

a. Fundamental Right
b. Legal Right
c. Fundamental Duity
d. None of the above

5. Universal Declaration of Human Rights was adopted on

a. 1 December 1947
b. 10 December 1948
c. 13 December 1950

d. None of the above

6. Who defined democracy as 'the Govt. of the People by the People and for the People'?

a. Mahatma Gandhi
b. Nelson Mandela
c. Ibrahim Lincoln
d. None of the above

7. Who criticised democracy

a. Mahatma Gandhi
b. Jhawarlal Nehru
c. Plato
d. None of the above

8. Modern Democracy is based on

a. Representative Democracy
b. Direct Democracy
c. Both a and b
d. None of the above

9. Which of the following country is known as largest democratic country of world

a. China
b. India
c. Russia
d. North Korea

10. Democracy originated in which of following country

a. China

b. Russia
c. Greece
d. USA

Answer Key

1. (c) 2. (d) 3. (a) 4. (b) 5. (b)
6. (c) 7. (c) 8. (a) 9. (b) 10. (c)

Exercise for practice

Short answer type questions

Q1. Define equality in your own words?
Q2. Define proportionate equality?
Q3. Define Liberty?
Q4. Write a note on the J. S. Mill's concept of liberty?
Q5. Define Liberty? Explain in brief the T. H. Green ideas on it?
Q6. Define Justice and explain it in your own words?
Q7. Discuss the liberal perspective of Justice?
Q8. Discuss the Marxist Perspective of Justice?
Q9. Define democracy? Explain in brief its evolution?
Q10. Define the following terms

a. Referendum
b. Initiative
c. Plebiscite
d. Recall

Q11. 'Democracy is government by the people of the people and for the people' Comment?

Long Answer Type Questions

Q1. Define Liberty? Discuss its negative and positive aspects?

Q2. Discuss the concept of justice? Explain in brief the social and economic concept of justice?

Q3. What do you know about democracy? Explain its features?

Q4. Define Equality? Explain its dimensions?

CHAPTER FOUR

MAJOR IDEOLOGIES

Liberalism: Classical, Modern and Contemporary

Liberalism

The term liberty and liberalism both are derived from the same Latin root 'liber' which means to liberate. So the basic idea beyond liberalism is to liberate the individual, to make him free from the restrain of state. Liberalism sought freedom of the individual in order to promote self-directing power of personality. Liberalism is a broad term it also includes the individualism and democracy.

Earlier exponents of the liberalism include John Locke, Adam Smith and Bentham. Locke is known as father of liberalism, Adam Smith is known as father of economics and Bentham is known as father of utilitarianism. They are the founder of classical liberalism or also called negative liberalism because it contemplates the negative role of the state. They believe that human being is rational, he has the capacity to develop his personality so the state should not restrict him otherwise he will not be able to develop himself properly.

Some writers trace its origin to the 17th century. This ideology was so popular that it dominated the western world for about four centuries. In 18th and 19th centuries it reached in its golden stage and accelerated the development of the western countries to a great extent. L. T. Hobhouse in his book 'Liberalism' have discussed certain basic principles which evolved as a consequences of the struggle of the middle class against the feudalism, the government by aristocracy and the power of clergy. Liberalism treats **'state as a**

necessary evil'. Which means that state is necessary as it provides security to the individuals and evil as it places certain restrictions on them.

Basic tenets of Liberalism:

- Man is a rational creature.
- There is no contradiction between individual self interest and common interest of state.
- Man is blessed with certain natural rights by nature which no form of govt. can take away.
- Liberalism promotes civil liberties of the individual including freedom of speech and expression, freedom of association and movement etc.
- Liberalism treats state a means and individual as an end.
- Liberalism holds freedom of contract.

Broadly speaking liberalism developed into three streams i.e *Classical Liberalism Or Negative Liberalism,*

Modern Liberalism Or Positive Liberalism and Contemporary Liberalism or Neo-Classical or Libertarianism.

Classical Liberalism: It is also known as negative liberalism. Its early exponents are John Lock (1632-1704), Adam Smith (1723-90), Jeremy Bentham (1748-1832) and John Stuart Mill (1806-73). All of them were English philosophers. Lock is known as father of liberalism. Adam Smith is known as father of economics and Bentham is known as father of utilitarianism. They advocate the policy of laissez Faire. They are the founder of classical liberalism which is called negative liberalism because it advocates the negative role of the state in the sphere of mutual dealings of individuals.

John Lock in his work 'Second treatise of civil government' argued that human beings are equal by nature and no individual can be placed under the authority of another except by his own consent. He believed that **'man is a rational being'**.

Adam Smith in his work 'Inquiry into the Nature and causes of the wealth of nations' argued that **"everyone has a natural**

prosperity to trade"andif given free rein this tendency will stimulate economic activity resulting in an increase in the production of goods. This profit motive is a natural instinct which inspires every trader to expand his business.

Bentham criticised the Locke that absolute right and absolute justice has no relevance to the realities of the social life. He criticised his concept of **natural rights as nonsense** and stressed that any policy of the state should be judged by the principle of 'greatest happiness of greatest number'. It is known as utilitarianism.

Modern Liberalism: It is a development in the concept of liberalism during the late nineteenth and early twentieth century. It is also known as positive liberalism because it focuses on positive role of state in the liberty and welfare of the people particularly the poor section. This concept of liberty was mainly to improve the condition of working class. The demand made by classical liberalism for the political rights and economic freedom for middle class had already achieved by the time. The condition of working class was bad so they updated the classical liberalism to modern liberalism in order to support the workers. Mill in his work '**Utilitarianism**' made a departure from negative liberalism on by two points

- Making a distinction between self regarding actions and other regarding actions and allowed the intervention of state only in other regarding actions
- By introducing a qualitative difference between different pleasures.

T. H. Green another English philosopher sought to add moral dimension to liberalism and thus advanced a full fledge theory of the welfare state. This stream of liberalism was further developed by other English philosophers such as L. T. Hobhouse, Harold J. Laski and R. H. Tawney. The welfare state also undertook labour welfare legislation involving fixed working hours, weekly rest and social security during old age, disability or death of the bread winner etc.

Features of positive liberalism

- It has firm faith in the rights and liberty of the individuals, enjoyed in a free and open society.
- Liberty is positive in character and has a social dimension.
- It believes in regulated and planned economy in the overall interest of the society.
- Liberty and equality are complementary to each other.
- Democracy and socialism are complementary to each other.
- Modern liberals put emphasis on groups rather than on individual.
- It has faith in constitutional, democratic and parliamentary system of government.

Contemporary Liberalism: It is also known as Neo-liberalism, Neo-classical Liberalism or libertarianism. It seeks to restore laissez-faire individualism. It denounces welfare state and opposes state intervention and control of economic activities. This theory criticizes the modern liberalism because of its welfare character. They believe that welfare state is opposite to individual liberty as it advocates the forced transfer of resources from more competent to less competent. The chief exponents of contemporary liberalism are F. A. Hayek (1899-1992), Milton Freedman (1912-2006) and Robert Nozick (1938-2002).

As we know the aim of the modern liberalism was to improve the condition of the working class but it failed to achieve this target. Instead of improving the condition of workers in welfare state their condition became worse. Various thinkers such as Karl Marx criticised the liberalism and suggested the socialism for improving condition of workers. In order to avoid such criticism various thinkers modified it from modern to contemporary liberalism.

In order to restore individual liberty, they sought to revive the principle of laissez-faire not only in economic sphere but also in social and political sphere. In a nutshell, neo-liberalism upholds full autonomy and freedom of the individual. It seeks his liberation from all institutions which tend to restrict his vision of the world, including the institutions of religion, family and customs of social conformity apart from political institutions. It focuses on Liberalization, Privatisation and globalization.

Robert Nozick believed that the function of the state should be reduced to only to provide security and hence treated state as a **night watchman**. He even criticised the taxation of rich for the welfare of the poor by the state.

Socialism: Evolutionary (Fabian)

Socialism is an economic system under which the major instruments of social production are placed under the ownership and control of public authority in order to ensure that they are properly utilized to secure the public interest.

Definitions

According to **Encyclopaedia Britannica** "socialism is that policy or theory, which aims at securing by the action of democratic authority a better distribution and in due subordinates thereto, a better production of wealth than now prevails".

Harold Laski "socialism implies such a control of the production and distribution of wealth as will enable the average citizens to have access to the resources, material and spiritual, which enable him, at least potentially to be himself at his best".

Schaffle "the Alpha and Omega of socialism is the transformation of private and competing capitalist into united collective capital".

Hubert Bland "Socialism is the common holding of the means of production and exchange and holding of them for the benefit of all".

Bernard Shaw "Socialism means the equality of income and nothing else".

Sellars defined socialism as "a democratic movement whose purpose is the securing of an economic organization of society which will give maximum at one time of justice and liberty".

J P Narayan Socialism means "a classless society in which all are workers".

Evolution of socialism

Socialism had evolved through history and Karl Max converted it from utopian socialism to scientific socialism. It evolved through following important steps;

- Saint Simmon (1760-1828) & Louis Blanc in France they advocated a centralized economy under state control.
- Robert Oven (1771-1858) in England and Charles Fourier in France produced plan for setting up model communities of free co-operation & free competition.
- J P Proudhon (1809-1865) in France hopes for setting up a national wide system of decentralized workers.
- These above all are known as utopian socialism.
- During beginning of 1830's and 1840's the idea of utopian socialism was criticized mainly by Karl Marx and Engel,
- They provided an alternative system of socialism known as scientific socialism.

Revolutionary Socialism

It made its appearance in Europe toward the close of 19th century as a reaction against revolutionary concept of Marxism. After the death of Karl Marx in 1883 his followers got divided into two schools. One school believed in orthodox or revolutionary method and the other believed in evolutionary method or revisionist. This 2nd group is called evolutionary socialism. The chief exponents of this school were Edward Bernstein, Jean Jaures, Edward Anseele, Bernard Shaw, Sydney Webb, Graham Wallas and G D H Cole.

Revolutionary socialism seeks to transform the social system thoroughly but evolutionary socialism admits an attitude of compromise between capitalism and socialism, so that the capitalist system is allowed to continue with some changes here and there in the socialist direction.

It is also known as Fabian socialism. Fabianism was first developed in England by the Fabinian society founded in 1884. The term 'Fabian' was adopted after the name of great Roman General, Quintus Fabius, whose tactics in the fight against Hannibal served as a guide for the society.

Revolutionary socialism or Marxian Socialism or Scientific Socialism:

It seeks to transform the social system thoroughly instead of accepting small concessions for the under privileged sections. It makes a direct attack on the prevailing conditions of the social order. This concept of socialist was given by Karl Marx and is also known as Marxian socialism. His early work mostly focuses values and is known as young Marxism. This early work was discovered and published after his death.

Main principles of Marxism

Marxism is the name given to the teaching of German political thinker Karl Mark. His supporters are known as Marxist thinkers. He has given following concepts in his scientific socialism

1. Dialectical Materialism: The word 'dialectic' originates from a Greek word 'dilego' which means dialogue or discussion. Plato used it as a method of discussion. Karl Marx borrowed this concept from Hegel and modified it to increase its relevance in his own thought. Hegel was of the view that idea or consciousness was the essence of universe. All the development in this world takes place in a zigzag manner. He gives three concepts i.e. Thesis, anti-thesis and synthesis.

When an initial idea or proposition called thesis, which don't represent truth clashes with anti-thesis which is just opposite or a negation of thesis and also doesn't represent the truth, it results in the formation of synthesis. This synthesis represents the true idea of both the thesis and antithesis, by destroying or negating their untruth element. This synthesis may not be complete true so it again takes the shape of thesis and clashes with its opponent, anti-thesis resulting in another synthesis. This process of negation of negation repeats again and again till it reaches the stage of absolute idea which is free from contradiction.

Hegel believes that the social institutions represent the idea and it is the dialectic process which is responsible for the development of social institutions.

Marx borrows the concept of thesis, anti-thesis and synthesis but without the concept of idealism and combines it with the materialism. Hence his dialectic method is known as dialectic materialism. He claims that the social institutions represent the material conditions and the dialectical materialism is responsible for the change in these institutions.

He favours that it was not idea which is important but it is the material or economic forces which are important. The development takes place in zigzag way by thesis, anti-thesis and synthesis of materialism. Following the concept of Hegel, Marx modified it and gave the concept that 'matter' was the essence of the universe, which embodies the force beyond all manifestation of social change.

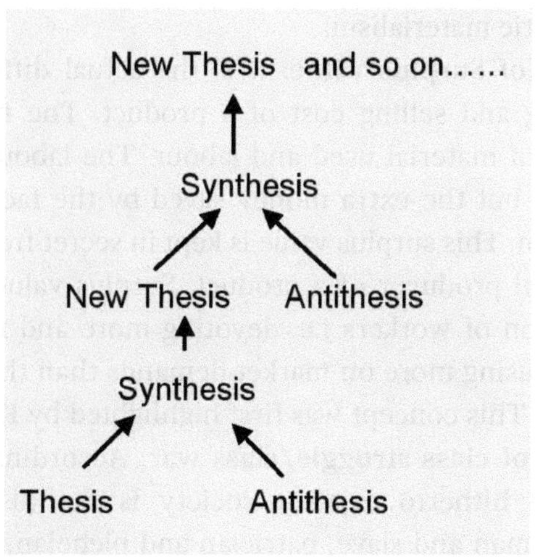

2. Economic or Materialistic Interpretation of History: According to Mark, production is the most important of all the human activities. The causes of social and political changes are to be found in the materialistic condition of the life. All the historic changes are determined by the means of production. Change in the means of production produces the change in the social, political and religious etc. dimensions. The economic factors are the most important determinant of other relations in the society. It represents the base of the society and other factors such as political, social and religious represents the super structure. We must make revolutionary change in base it will automatically change super structure. He divided history into four stages;

- Primitive Communism
- Ancient society
- Feudal society
- Capitalist society

The reason beyond the growth of society from primitive communism to capitalist society through ancient and feudal society was the dialectic materialism.

3. Theory of Surplus value: It is the actual difference in the manufacturing and selling cost of a product. The manufacturing cost consists of material used and labour. The labour cost is paid to the worker but the extra money saved by the factory owner is kept with them. This surplus value is kept in secret from the worker who is the real producer of a product. Surplus value is generated by the violation of workers i.e. devoting more and more working hours and focusing more on market demands than the real interest of worker etc. This concept was first highlighted by Karl Mark.

4. Theory of class struggle/class war: According to Marx the history of all hitherto existing society is the history of class struggle; free man and slave, patrician and plebeian, lord and serf, guild master and journey man. He says that in every society there are two classes of people i.e. haves and haves not. Haves are those controlling means of production and distribution whereas haves not are those having no control on means of production and distribution. Haves not are mainly the working class having no other way to survive except selling their physical labour. This division of the society into two classes, results in a revolution and revolution removes this division by giving the opportunity to those who were not having any control on means of production. With this process society moves toward progress. He believes that the present hostility between bourgeois and proletariat shall ultimately end with the victory of the workers

5. Theory of revolution: According to Marx in this present capitalist system of state the condition of workers is bad. To improve their condition we must have to over through this capitalist system. He believes that this system of state is established and adjusted by the bourgeois i.e. capitalist class for the domination of the working class. As long as the state exists there are no chances of getting justice. Karl Marx and Engels in their work ***'Communist Manifesto'*** made calls to all the workers of the world to unite to over overthrow this system of capitalism and establishment of a classless society. They gave a call to all the workers of the world to unite as they have nothing to lose except the chains in their hand and a world to win. Marx first of all suggest the constitutional method for the revolution but if it is not possible the workers can even go through revolutionary methods to over through the capitalism. This call for revolution by Marx has inspired many minds which resulted into Russian as well as Chinese revolution.

6. Dictatorship of Preliterate: The ultimate aim of the Karl Marx is abolition of state and establish a class society but this could not be attained straight way. For this he envisaged the phase of dictatorship of preliterate as a transitional stage. In this phase the workers will use even revolution to over through the capitalists. In this phase the state will not wither away and the workers will make the use of this state machinery to crush the capitalists and other opposing elements to communism. The state shall be used to abolish private property, socialise the means of transportation and industries etc. It will be the dictatorship of the workers, for the crushing evens the last remains of capitalists. Once the workers will succeed in over throwing the capitalists, the state will automatically wither away because it was formed by capitalists for their personal benefit.

7. Stateless and classless society: According to Mark, when the dictatorship of preliterate stage will be established, then state will wither away and the society will become classless. The workers will work in dictatorship of proletariat to crushing evens the last remains of capitalists. Once the workers will succeed in over throwing the capitalists, the state will automatically wither away because it was formed by capitalists for their personal benefit. The revolution will finally land in its final stage i.e. a classless society. It will be stable as there will be no class and hence no chances of revolution.

8. Religion: He gives more importance to religion and highlights its negative effects. He said the 'religion is the opium of the people'. The capitalist use this religion to make a belief among the workers that the God has made their destiny as working class and the God is responsible to their condition and not any other class such as capitalists. This is the reason that communist countries today avoid any dominance of religion among their citizens and place more focus on physical work for growth of their nation.

Criticism of Marxism: Various thinkers claim that the socialist philosophy has lost its relevance because of various changes in the world. His whole concept was based on the revolution by working class but in contemporary class there are more technicians than workers in this world. Today more people are in the service field that as workers. Communist counties have reduced freedom to their citizens in the contemporary world. China has applied the socialist concept in their country but its revolutionary class was not the workers but were the peasants.

Secularism: Western and Indian Perspectives

Secularism: Secularism is defined as the separation of state from the influence and functioning of all religious institutions. Secular means a state must not only refuse to be theocratic but also have no formal, legal alliance with any religion. The separation of religion-state is, however, a necessary but not a sufficient ingredient of a secular state.

A secular state must be committed to principles and goals which are at least partly derived from non-religious sources. These ends should include peace, religious freedom and freedom from religiously grounded oppression, discrimination and exclusion, as also inter-religious and intra-religious equality. All secular states have one thing in common: they are neither theocratic nor do they establish a religion.

Depending upon their distance with religion secularism is divided into two types 1st represented by USA and is known as Western Secularism and the other represented by India known as Indian Secularism.

Western Secularism: This concept of secularism came first in mid 17th Century by the Enlightenment movement and first enshrined in the Constitution of France followed by French Revolution 1789. In this type of Secularism, State is separated from the functioning of all religious groups and institutions.

The State treats all religions with equal indifference. It does not aid any religious institutions. The State believes in total non-interference of religion. The state is allowed to curtail the rights of citizens if the religion is causing hindrance in the functioning of the State. The state will not intervene in the affairs of religion and, in the same manner religion will not interfere in the affairs of the state.

Indian Prospective: The nature of Indian secularism is different from that of western secularism. Although, religion is considered separate from politics in India. In individual life religion is accepted. The positive concept of secularism developed in India states that the state should adhere to this principle without any political use of religion.

Thus, despite the greatness of India, the integrity of the nation has been maintained. Secularism has no alternative option in a multicultural nation like India therefore, the Indian Constitution adopted secularism. People of different languages and religions live in Indian Union. They needed secularism to keep them together. Therefore, with the right to freedom, it was necessary to accept secularism.

There is no mention of word secularism in Indian Constitution except in Preamble. The word secular in Preamble was too added in 1974. But India was also a secular state before 1974. Indian secularism does not focus only on church-state separation and the idea of inter-religious equality is crucial to the Indian conception.

Feminism: Meaning, Types and Issues

Feminism is an ideology that demands the equal status and rights for women as per men in society. Feminism is a branch of thought which deals with the condition of women in the society, the cause of their suffering and measures for restoring their power, position and wealth. They hold that women have suffered a long and are still suffering injustice because of their sex.

They are of the view that in political sphere the condition of women has improved a little bit but in domestic sphere their position is still moribund. Feminist activists have campaigned for women's rights such as in contract property and voting etc.

Feminism is the advocacy of women's rights on the grounds of equality of sexes. This philosophy of feminism originated from the western world and spread to all corner of world.

E. C. Stanton, Mary Wollstonecraft, J. S. Mill, Harriet Taylor, Simone de Beauvoir, J. A. Tickner and Kate Chopin etc. are some of the feminist writers. Depending upon the type of feminist ideology it is of so many types. Broadly it is divided into three types as given below.

Types of Feminism

There are three types of Feminism i.e. Liberalism Feminism, Socialist Feminism and Radical Feminism.

a. **Liberalism Feminism:** It represents the earliest trend of feminism. It demands uplift the status and condition of women in society under the banner of liberalism. It focuses on achieving gender equality through political and legal reforms within the framework of liberal democracy. This type of the feminism had its roots in USA and Britain. In USA figures such as E. C. Stanton and Susan Anthony raised the issue of women freedom and equality as a result in anti-slavery movements. They both edited a feminist journal "The Revolution". The British liberal feminism appeared to have its greatest triumph when all women become eligible to vote in 1928. In other countries it was achieved later. Liberalism Feminism has also been criticised mainly by radical feminist thinkers. They believe that liberal feminism is too superficial in its approach.

b. **Socialist Feminist:** This branch of feminism too criticise the liberal feminism. This branch mainly supports the position of working class women and the problem they have with exploitation and poor conditions in the workplace. Marxist feminists in particular want to challenge the view of the state as a benevolent reformer and to argue that the state is an expression of the class domination. The freedom of women has to be linked to the emancipation of the working class in general, with a much greater concentration on the social and economic dimension of gender discrimination. Rosa Luxemburg has worked more in social feminist branch in general and Marx feminism in particular.

c. **Radical Feminism:** It is a prospective within feminism that demands for a radical reordering of the society in which male superiority is eliminated in all social, economic and political contexts. Men not only oppose women but they are responsible for war, violence, hierarchy and the exploitation of nature and their fellow beings. Radical see themselves as sexual revolutionaries. They believe that women are oppressed because women are women and men are men. Male domination permeates all aspects of society ranging from sports, literature, dress, philosophy, Army and entertainment to sexual mores. They argue that the basis of women's oppression lies with childbearing, as well as rearing and the conception of love. Women in the view of radical feminist do not want equality with men. They want liberation, and liberation is only possible if patriarchy is overthrown.

Women's Issues: Welfare to Empowerment

Women Issues: The position of women in different Societies is different, but one thing is common that in every society they are dominated by their male partners. In almost all the societies they were given very less importance. In developed countries of the west, women are in a little bit good position but they are supposed to be weak as compare to male.

During the election campaign of US President, Hillary Clinton was supposed to be weak before the Donald Trump and this was the main reason she was defeated in election of President Candidate. In ancient India, women were respected as mother, sister and daughters. They were treated as Goddess. With the passage of time and frequent invasions by invaders, they lost their respect in the society.

During the Mahabharata, Drupadi was divided by Pandas as common wife and also miss behaved by Kauroes. In modern India too, the condition of women is not good. The Shah Bano case, Nirbhaya rape case etc are its live examples. India is one of the top most countries having women insecurity. National commission for women in India released a data in 2015 showing that half of the rape cases in India are from the state of Utter Pradesh.

In addition to this Indian's women were not weak. India is a home of various lioness women such as late Miss Vijay Lakshmi Pandit, Late Mrs Indra Gandhi, Late Mother Terisa, Late Kalpna Chawla, Mrs Sonia Gandhi, Miss Sunita William and Mrs Patiba Devi Singh Patal etc.

Following are the some of the women issues:

a. **Issue of Child Marriage:** Today also female are being married much before their maturity. It results in increase in the population of country and the bad condition of women in society.

b. **Issue of polygamy:** The women in India are also affected badly by the polygamy. Now a day women in Muslim as well as tribal community are facing this problem.
c. **Right to Divorce:** Govt. of India has passed Tripple Talaq Bill restricting more than one marriage and making divorce a tough process for Muslim communities.
d. **Issue of Dowry:** It a major cause for poverty in various states of India such as Utter Pradesh, Bihar, Gujarat and Rajasthan etc. The Govt. has failed to check this ill practice in Society.
e. **Issue of Right to Property:** In this Patriarchal Society women are denied property rights. With this they get no share in the property of their parents.
f. **Continuous Rapes in India:** This is a matter of shame for a country whose history clearly shows that females were worshiped in the form of Goddess. Today girls are not safe outside their homes in any corner of India. Nirbhaya rape case in Delhi and Gudia rape case of Shimla etc. are some of its live examples. The condition has become so worse that even female animals such as Bitch, Goat etc. are not safe in India.

Some of the positive steps for women empowerment are given below;

a. **Sati was abolished in 1829:** It is seen as a major development in the path of women empowerment
b. **Bharat Street Maha Mandal:** It is a self help group made by women. This group has played an important role in the development of women in India.
c. **Women Indian association 1917:** It is also a self help group made by women. This group has also played an important role in the development of women in India.
d. **All India women conference 1927:** It is a Non-Governmental Organization formed by Margaret Cousins at Delhi in 1927. It has worked more for education of women and children.

e. **National Commission for women 1990:** It is a statutory body of Government of India. Its main aim is to advise the government on all policy matters affecting women.

From Welfare to Empowerment: 42nd amendment in 1976 added a fundamental duty for dignity of women in art 51A. National policy for improvement of women was formed in 2001. In 16th Lok Sabha elections, 61 women were elected. The women stated their journey by demanding for their welfare but today they are struggling for empowerment.

Following are some of the points claiming for their demands of empowerment.

a. **Entry in Sabrimala Temple:** This temple is situation in Kerala. Women from the reproductive age group were not allowed to visit this temple. In 2006 six women filled a petition to lift the ban against entering of 10 – 50 years age women. In 2018 Supreme Court of India agreed on it.
b. **Mee Too Movement:** It is a social movement against the sexual abuse and sexual harassment where people publicize allegation of sex crime committed with them. Women mostly avoid disclosing any misbehaved incident with them to anybody due to cultural curtains particularly in India. Mee Too movement clearly shows the confidence of women to publicize allegation of sex crime committed with them.
c. **Tripple Talaq Movement:** Various women started protesting against this Tripple Talaq malpractice in Muslim Community. The Government was forced to take action and as a result of which Govt. of India passed Tripple Talaq Bill.
d. **Women in Army, Navy and Air force:** Today women are performing well in all three branches of Indian Defence forces. Women have got permanent commission even in Indian Army. They are flying the fighter jets equally with men Pilots.
e. **Reservation for women in PRI bodies:** After the 33% reservation for women in Panchayati Raj Institutions various

women are taking part in PRI politics. With this they have become more aware and empowered.

Women at International Level: Indian Women are shining ranging from Space to Sports. Astronuants such as Sunita William, Lt. Kalpna Chawla & Sports persons such as Shakshi Malik, Merry Com etc. are its live examples.

Gender in International Politics:

The Millennium Development Goals (MDG) upholds gender equality and women's empowerment and respective goals for achieving them. The Millennium Project Task Force on Gender education has developed a framework that why gender equality is so important to each of the MDGs.

Human Development Index (HDI) gave a new dimension to the development by considering factors or indicators, other than the economic one. It includes the basic dimensions of human development health, knowledge and living standards. It however does not reveal the disparity of development between females and males.

Therefore keeping in view the same component of HDI, the United Nation Development Programme (UNDP) formulated a Gender Development Index (GDI) in its report in 1995. It is the ratio of the HDI calculated separately for males and females using the same methodology as for HDI. It shows the gender gap by showing females HDI as a percentage of Male HDI.

Gender gap reveals the percentage of under-development of females in the three indicator areas i.e. health, knowledge and living standards as compared to their male counterparts. The GDI is calculated at present for 166 countries which grouped into five categories based on the absolute deviation from the gender priority in HDI values i.e.

a) Very High Human Development
b) High Human Development
c) Medium Human Development
d) Low Human Development

e) Other Countries or territories

Along with GDI, another measure which is used to calculate gender inequality is Gender Inequality Index (GII) which is introduced in 2010 by United National Development Programme. Another important indicator of gender development is Gender Empowerment Measure (GEM). It was introduced by UNDP Human Development Report of 1995.

This uses estimated earned income based on non-agriculture wages, percentage of parliamentary seats by gender percentage of technical position held by women and percentage of legislators, senior officials and managers who are women as indicators. The three dimensions considered in GEM are

a. Political participation and decision making
b. Economic participation and decision making
c. Power over economic resources

The index in this GEM runs from 0 to 1 with 1 being the maximum.

India ranked 129 in Human Developed Index, whereas Sri Lanka ranked and China ranked 71 and 85 respectively. India's Gender Development Index is 0.819 which is much less as compared to 0.913, the average GDI of developing Countries.

The role of gender in international politics was clearly defined by J. Ann Tickner a professor of Colombia University, feminist thinker in her book 'Gender in International politics'. She says that men's duty as a member of a Commonwealth is to assist in maintenance, in the advance, in the defence of the state. The women's duty as the member of the Commonwealth is to assist in the ordering, in the comforting and in the beautiful adornment of the state.

Conclusion: It can be concluded from the above discussion that India is the largest democratic country but still it lacks in Gender equality as compared to its neighbouring small countries. India ranks 129 in Human Development Index which is very bad as compared to the condition of Sri Lanka and China

Multiple Choice Questions

1. Who gave the concept of 'Utilitarianism'

a. J. S. Mill
b. Jeremy Bentham
c. Hobbes
d. None of the above

2. 'Utilitarianism' is the work of which of the following thinkers

a. Jeremy Bentham
b. Karl Marx
c. J. S. Mill
d. J. J. Rousseau

3. 'Greatest good of the greatest number' was advocated by

a. Liberalism
b. Utilitarianism
c. Neo- Liberalism
d. Libertarianism

4. The credit of introducing far reaching changes in liberal philosophy goes to

a. J. S. Mill
b. T. H. Green
c. Laski
d. None of the above

5. In broad sense 'Liberalism' can be equated with

a. Socialism

b. Marxism
c. Leninism
d. Capitalism

6. Liberalism stands for

a. Social Liberty
b. Political Liberty
c. Economic Liberty
d. All of the above

7. Who among the following is known as father of liberal political philosophy

a. John Locke
b. Laski
c. Hobbes
d. None of the above

8. Liberalism which flourished in the seventeenth and 18th centuries is known as

a. Early Liberalism
b. Primitive Liberalism
c. Classical Liberalism
d. All of the above

9. Which of the following expounded the philosophy of 'Positive Liberalism'?

a. J. M. Robertson
b. H. J. Laski
c. J. A. Hobson
d. All of the above

10. 'Mao Tse Tung' belong to which of the following county

a. Russia
b. France
c. China
d. India

11. A famous Marxist 'Lenin' belongs to which of the following country

a. China
b. Japan
c. USA
d. *Russia*

Answer Key

1. (b) 2. (c) 3. (b) 4. (b) 5. (d)

6. (d) 7. (a) 8. (c) 9. (d) 10. (c)
11. (d)

Exercise for practice

Short answer type questions

Q1. Define Liberalism in simple words? What are its types?
Q2. What do you know about classical liberalism?
Q3. Define Neo-Liberalism?
Q4. Define utopian socialism?
Q5. What do you know about Anarchism? Was Gandhi Ji an Anarchist?
Q6. Define scientific socialism? How it was different from utopian socialism?
Q7. Write a note on the contribution of Karl Marx in Socialism?
Q8. Karl Marx was known as God by Half of World and Devil by another half? Comment?
Q9. Define Secularism? What are its types?

Q10. Define feminism? Explain the contribution of few feminist thinkers?

Q11. Define Feminism? Do you agree that Plato and J. S. Mill were Feminist thinkers?

Long Answer Type Questions

Q12. Explain the term Liberalism? Give its types in detail?

Q13. Define Secularism? Discuss Indian and western secularism? Suggest few measures to improve secularism in India?

Q14. Define Socialism? Discuss the contribution of Karl Marx in the field of socialism?

Q15. What do you know about the feminism? Discuss its types?

Q16. Define Feminism? Discuss Indian Feminism from welfare to empowerment?

9 798889 861249

Printed by Libri Plureos GmbH in Hamburg,
Germany